I0176507

"Wisdom That Transforms. Action That Lasts."

The Get Wisdom Commitment

At Get Wisdom Publishing we believe that true wisdom has the power to transform lives. Our mission is to equip readers with timeless insights and practical tools that inspire growth, guide decisions, and empower purposeful living. We don't just inform—we empower.

Our books combine profound understanding with real-life application, enabling readers to unlock their potential and navigate life's challenges with clarity and confidence. With each step guided by wisdom, we help you create lasting change and live the life you deserve.

When wisdom meets purpose, transformation follows.

The *OBSCURE*
Bible Study Series

Grow in your faith through investigating unusual and obscure biblical characters.

"Deep Biblical Wisdom.
Real-Life Faith Application."

The OBSCURE Bible Study Journey

Meet Shamgar, Jethro, Manoah & Hathach	4 Lessons
Blasphemy, Grace, Quarrels & Reconciliation	8 Lessons
The Beginning and the End	8 Lessons
God at the Center	8 Lessons
Women of Courage	8 Lessons
The Beginning of Wisdom	8 Lessons
Miracles and Rebellion	8 Lessons
The Chosen People	8 Lessons
The Chosen Person	8 Lessons

God at the Center

He is sovereign and I am not.

Personal Study Guide
Book 4

Deepen your faith.
Strengthen your walk.

Stephen H Berkey

GETWISDOM
PUBLISHING

COPYRIGHT

ISBN 978-1-952359-02-6   (Leader Guide, paperback)

ISBN 978-1-952359-03-3   (Leader Guide, ebook)

ISBN 978-1-952359-04-0   (Personal Study Guide, paperback)

ISBN 978-1-952359-05-7   (Personal Study Guide, ebook)

Audiobook available   (amazon.com and audible.com)

Bible Translations Used:

Discover the biblical characters that mainstream studies forget – and the timeless lessons they teach."

TABLE OF CONTENTS

CONTENTS

FREE PDF RESOURCES

Living Wisely
The Life Planning Guide

A Quick-Start Guide to Purposeful Living and Wise Decisions!

Discover the five life domains: purpose, people, principles, productivity, and perspective. Wisdom is the ability to apply truth and logic to real-life decisions and produce good outcomes. It influences your choices and will produce action that lasts. Consider and apply the five practical wisdom principles for daily living. (6 pages)

Free PDF: https://getwisdompublishing.com/resource-registration/

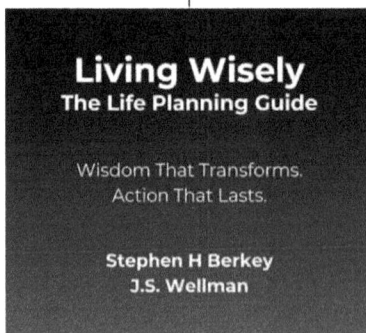

Living Wisely
The Life Planning Guide

Wisdom That Transforms.
Action That Lasts.

Stephen H Berkey
J.S. Wellman

Free PDF

Five Practical Principles For Life

When wisdom meets purpose, transformation follows.

Free PDF
Wise Decision-Making

[Get the ebook version for 99 cents]

You can make good choices.

This free resource provides a project-oriented perspective and gives ten detailed steps to analyze issues/problems to determine a solution. (26 pages)

Good decisions expand your horizons. Don't allow the fear of decision-making paralyze your ability to make good choices. Think through the reasonable alternatives and move forward. When your eyes are on the goal, making good decisions is easier.

Free PDF: https://getwisdompublishing.com/resource-registration/

Kindle ebook for 99 cents: https://www.amazon.com/dp/B09SYGWRVL/

Ebook

Free PDF

Make Thoughtful Decisions!

Good decisions expand your horizons.

Why Study OBSCURE Characters?

Unique, New, and Fresh

For experienced Bible students these characters will provide a fresh and interesting approach to Bible study. Since most of the material will be unfamiliar to the participants, new believers or those just starting Bible study should not feel intimidated by students who have been studying for years. Most readers will not be acquainted with the majority of the characters and events in this series.

Knowledge of Scripture

These studies are a great introduction for those just beginning Bible study. Regardless of their level of knowledge, everyone should find the characters and stories provide an opportunity to grow in their faith through investigating fascinating and unusual biblical stories and incidents.

Valuable Life Lessons

These lesser-known characters are a lot like you and me. God uses all sorts of people to accomplish His plans! You will become familiar with ordinary people, strange characters, and people living on the fringe of life who have the same troubles and challenges as people today. The deep truths and life lessons embedded in these studies should be valuable. They will provide new insights to scripture.

"Unlock Biblical Wisdom.
Transform Your faith!"

ABOUT THE LEADER GUIDE

All of the books in this Bible Study series have an extensive Leader Guide. If you are a participant in a group, a Leader Guide is not necessary, unless you want the author's answers. If you are studying independently, you may want the Leader Guide.

In the Guide the answers follow the questions with a small amount of space for the Leader's personal responses. If you are using the Leader Guide and want to do the study without the influence of the author's answers the best solution is to obtain the blank Worksheets, which are free. This will allow you to record your answers separately before reviewing the answers in the Leader Guide.

See the instructions on the previous "FREE RESOURCES" page to access the free Worksheets.

"Discover the Overlooked.
Apply it to Your Life!"

Book Description

Are you longing for a deeper connection with God but feel stuck in the chaos of life?

Do you know God is real, yet sometimes struggle to *feel* His presence? Does anxiety creep in, even when you know He's in control?

"God at the Center" invites you to re-center your life around the One who holds it all together. This study helps you gain a deeper, more personal relationship with God by applying His Word to your daily life. Discover the keys to effective prayer, learn that you can pray with boldness, and unlock a clearer sense of purpose and direction as you align yourself with His divine calling.

Explore the lives of Joseph, the sinful woman, the potter, and the virgins who ran out of oil, discovering practical steps to re-center your life with the Lord as the focus. Step out and know the Lord in every moment of your day. Don't let another day pass without experiencing God's Word anew.

Book 4 in the OBSCURE series looks at eight different characters whose stories reveal God at the very center of their lives. The virgin birth is investigated through Joseph, the husband of Mary. True worship and God's forgiveness are observed in the story of the sinful woman who anointed Jesus' feet with her tears. God's sovereignty is the focus of the stories about the potter and Ananias and his wife Sapphira, who died after their lies were exposed.

We observe the nature and characteristics of the prayer of Jabez and consider whether our personal prayers are big enough. Are we praying prayers that have eternal significance?

The study of Zophar, one of Job's "friends," provides an opportunity to reflect on the Retribution Principle. This principle is foundational to understanding many of the proverbs in the Bible: if I do good things, I will receive good in return, and if I do bad things, I will receive bad things in return.

The book wraps up with lessons on the parable of the ten virgins and the story of Jesus and the woman at the well in Samaria. The parable of the ten virgins tells us that we must be prepared and ready, because the bridegroom could return at any time. It also makes it clear that we must have a relationship with Christ.

Knowing about Jesus is not sufficient; we must truly know Him. Last we examine the circumstances surrounding Jesus' conversation with the Samaritan woman at Jacob's Well. Jesus described living water and said that everyone who drank water from the well would be thirsty again, but the water He would give would become a well of water "springing up to eternal life." The woman rightly perceived that Jesus is the Messiah and rushed into the town to tell the leaders what she saw and heard. That raises the question, "Have I rightly discerned who Jesus is and what did I do with that information?"

"Scripture holds answers in unexpected places. Our unique Bible studies reveal overlooked wisdom for today's challenges."

INTRODUCTION

We equip readers with timeless wisdom and practical tools that transform, not just inform. Our books combine deep insights with real-life application to create lasting change.

Description of The OBSCURE Bible Study Series

This unique series uses a number of lesser-known Bible characters and events to explore such major themes as Angels, being Born Again, Courage, Death, Evangelism, Faithfulness, Forgiveness, Grace, Hell, Leadership, Miracles, the Remnant, the Sabbath, Salvation, Rebellion, Sovereignty, Thankfulness, Women, the World, Creation, and End Times.

The series as a whole provides both a broad and fresh understanding of the nature of God as we see Him act in the lives of people we've never examined before.

Most of the people chosen for these studies are unfamiliar because they are mentioned only a few times in Scripture – fifteen only once or twice. Others, although more familiar, are included because of their particular contribution to kingdom work.

For example, Scripture mentions Shamgar only twice. One verse in Judges 3:31 tells his story and 5:6 simply establishes a timeline and says nothing more about him. Then there is Nicodemus, with whom we associate the concept of being "born again." His name appears only 5 times, all in one short passage in the book of John. Eve, although obviously not obscure, is included in order to investigate the creation story.

Group Discussion or Individual Study

These studies can be done individually or in a small discussion group. The real value of the study is in the discussion questions. We all see life differently and the thoughts and ideas shared in a group will often lead to a richer understanding of the Scripture. The questions often require the participant to put himself (herself) in the mind or circumstances of that person in the Scriptures.

The commentary portion of the introductory material in each lesson is there to help clarify the passage and set the stage for the discussion questions. The questions are designed to help the student understand the meaning of the text itself and explore the kingdom implications from a personal point of view.

Ideal For Both New and Mature Bible Students

These lessons have three underlying questions:

- "Who is this person?"
- "What is happening here?"
- "What is the implication for my life?"

Because of the obscurity of the characters under study, chances are that even experienced participants with prior understanding of the lesson's theme will find fresh material to explore. Both new and long-time students will be challenged by the life lessons these unfamiliar characters can teach them.

Format of Lessons

Each lesson begins with the Scripture using the ESV translation followed by short sections titled "Context," "What Do We Know," and "Observations." The discussion questions are designed to help the student understand the subject and are followed by several application questions.

"We believe applied wisdom empowers life change. Our books provide clarity, inspiration, and tools to equip readers to live their best life."

Joseph
husband of Virgin Mary

Occurrences of "Joseph" in the Bible: 14

Themes: Virgin birth; Dreams

Note: Three of the fourteen mentions of Mary's husband, Joseph, are in John and they identify Jesus as the son of Joseph; four more are in Luke and confirm details already provided in Matthew.

Scripture

Joseph, husband of Mary
Matt 1:16   *and Jacob the father of Joseph the husband of Mary, of whom Jesus was born, who is called Christ.* ESV

The Birth of Jesus Christ
Matthew 1:18-25   *Now the birth of Jesus Christ took place in this way. When his mother Mary had been betrothed to Joseph, before they came together she was found to be with child from the Holy Spirit. 19 And her husband Joseph, being a just man and unwilling to put her to shame, resolved to divorce her quietly. 20 But as he considered these things, behold, an angel of the Lord appeared to him in a dream, saying, "Joseph, son of David, do not fear to take Mary as your wife, for that which is conceived in her is from the Holy Spirit. 21 She will bear a son, and you shall call his name Jesus, for he will save his people from their sins." 22 All this took place to fulfill what the Lord had spoken by the prophet:*

23 "Behold, the virgin shall conceive and bear a son, and they shall call his name Immanuel" (which means, God with us). 24 When Joseph woke from sleep, he did as the angel of the Lord commanded him: he took his wife, 25 but knew her not until she had given birth to a son. And he called his name Jesus. ESV

The Flight to Egypt

Matthew 2:13   *Now when they had departed, behold, an angel of the Lord appeared to Joseph in a dream and said, "Rise, take the child and his mother, and flee to Egypt, and remain there until I tell you, for Herod is about to search for the child, to destroy him."* ESV

The Return to Nazareth

Matt 2:19-23   *But when Herod died, behold, an angel of the Lord appeared in a dream to Joseph in Egypt, 20 saying, "Rise, take the child and his mother and go to the land of Israel, for those who sought the child's life are dead." 21 And he rose and took the child and his mother and went to the land of Israel. 22 But when he heard that Archelaus was reigning over Judea in place of his father Herod, he was afraid to go there, and being warned in a dream he withdrew to the district of Galilee. 23 And he went and lived in a city called Nazareth, that what was spoken by the prophets might be fulfilled: "He shall be called a Nazarene."* ESV

The Context

Marriage

In Jesus' day, an engaged couple did not live together – that was contrary to the prescribed normal behavior. Neither were they intimate during the "engagement" period, although they were referred to as husband and wife. Interestingly, the relationship could only be dissolved by an actual divorce. This engagement period normally lasted for about a year and was used to demonstrate the faithfulness of the parties, and specifically the promise of virginity given by the bride. If the bride was or became pregnant during this period the marriage could be annulled. If the bride was proven "pure" then the husband paraded to the home of his bride's parents and in a grand procession led his bride to their new home.

Joseph

Joseph's engagement turned out to be much different than he would have expected. There was no parade. There was no big community party with all the family, friends, and neighbors. Instead, there was stress! Joseph was told about the unique conditions of his engagement and marriage by an angel of the Lord in a dream. In fact, Joseph had four dreams in which he was given information and instruction about his marriage and his family. In all these situations Joseph was obedient and did as he was instructed.

What Do We Know?

Virgin Birth

It is significant to note that in Matthew 1:16 Mary was identified as the mother of Jesus and Joseph was described as the husband of Mary, not the father of Jesus. Matthew 1:19 specifically says that Joseph was not the biological father but that the Holy Spirit impregnated Mary. This was confirmed again in Matthew 1:20. Some people have difficulty believing in the virgin birth, but if you believe that the Holy Spirit (God) cannot impregnate Mary, then how can you believe any of the miracles and powers of God? Joseph, being the righteous and God-fearing man that he was, did exactly as God commanded. The text specifically says that Joseph did not have intimate relations with Mary until after Jesus was born.

Name

The angel of the Lord told Joseph to name the child "Jesus," because Jesus would save His people from their sins. The birth of Jesus fulfilled the prophecy in Isaiah 7:14 which Isaiah quoted in the text. Another name mentioned in the quote from Isaiah reveals that "Immanuel" means "God with us." Joseph obeyed, and named the child Jesus.

Warning in a dream
Again, the angel appeared to Joseph in a dream and told him to take his family to Egypt. Joseph complied immediately. After King Herod died, the angel appeared in another dream and told Joseph it was safe to return to Israel. Joseph was warned in yet another dream not to go into Judea, so he went to Nazareth in Galilee. Thus, Jesus can be referred to as a Nazarene.

Implications and Observations

Virgin birth: doctrine
The virgin birth is an important doctrinal fact that all Christians need to understand. The Messiah's birth was prophesied in the Old Testament to be to a virgin. There are several real and important reasons for this fact of Jesus' birth. Question B8 below asks you to determine these reasons. Most study Bibles, gospel commentaries, or Bible dictionaries will provide the answer.

Joseph was a righteous man
Joseph had to be a very special man! He would have needed great faith in both God and Mary. Even with great faith he would have had to wonder how this was all going to work out. He could easily have considered the possibility of becoming an outcast. And, how would he explain all this to his family and friends? Would he be a laughingstock of the village and the object of whispering and gossip? But Joseph trusted in God more than in his fears. Although his response may be amazing to us, God knew all along the fiber of the man He had chosen for Mary's husband.

Secret divorce
It would be reasonable, after reading Matthew 1:19, to wonder how it would be possible to divorce secretly in that day and age. Other translations use the word "quietly" rather than "secretly." It

could obviously not be done in total secrecy. Some people would have to know, but Joseph could go about the process so that no public spectacle occurred. It would have been Joseph's right to report her to the authorities and have her stoned to death (Dt 22:23-24).

Discussion Questions

GENERAL

A1. Must one believe in the virgin birth at the time of conversion?

A2. What would have been significant to Jewish readers in Matthew 1:16?

A3. What is the most striking fact or occurrence to you in this story, other than the virgin birth?

A4. If you had been either Joseph or Mary in this story, what would have been the most difficult aspect of the whole situation?

A5. In strictly human terms, what possible problems might the facts surrounding Jesus' birth have had on the marriage relationship between Joseph and Mary?

A6. How might Joseph have felt about being the "parent" of the Son of God or the Messiah?

Q. Would Joseph have thought Jesus was more than the "son of God"? Would he have had reason to think Jesus was the Messiah?

A7. What do we learn about our faith from this story of Joseph? How would you have reacted under these circumstances if you had been Joseph?

Q. How would you really have known it was God? How would you have known or confirmed it was God? Is there any information in Scripture that would have helped?

A8. The Greek form of Jesus is Joshua. What does "Joshua" mean?

Q. What do <u>you</u> think this name and its meaning would have meant to the people at that time?

A9. Why was Joseph told what to name the child and not Mary?

B. IMPLICATIONS

B1. What does verse Matthew 1:19 tell us about Joseph? What does it mean that he is a righteous man?

B2. What do you think were the motives behind Joseph's intent to divorce Mary quietly?

B3. What does verse Matthew 1:20 tell us about Joseph?

B4. In Matthew 1:21 what reason does the author give for Jesus' birth?

B5. What is the author's primary purpose in Matthew 1:22-23? NOTE: The book of Matthew was written primarily to the Jews.

B6. What do we learn about Joseph in Matthew 1:24?

B7. After the stories about Jesus' birth, Joseph is not mentioned by name again in Scripture. It is assumed he died during Jesus' youth. Assuming this was by design, what are the logical reasons why God might want Joseph out of the picture?

B8. Why must the Holy Spirit be the cause of the pregnancy and not Joseph? What doctrinal issue requires a "virgin birth"?

C. DREAMS

C1. How many dreams did Joseph have? Who spoke to him and what was he told to do?

C2. Why do you think Joseph believed these dreams without any reported questions about their validity?

C3. What were typical purposes of dreams and visions in the Bible?

D. APPLICATION

D1. Do you need to trust or obey God for something He is telling you to do?

D2. Is there something God is telling you to escape or flee from and you are delaying?

D3. Is there someone you need to protect or rescue?

D4. Have you been away and it is now time to return?

Sinful Woman
the repentant prostitute

Occurrences of "sinful woman" in the Bible: 1

Themes: Worship; Priorities

Scripture

Luke 7:36-50   *A Sinful Woman Forgiven*
36 One of the Pharisees asked him to eat with him, and he went into the Pharisee's house and took his place at the table. 37 And behold, a woman of the city, who was a sinner, when she learned that he was reclining at table in the Pharisee's house, brought an alabaster flask of ointment, 38 and standing behind him at his feet, weeping, she began to wet his feet with her tears and wiped them with the hair of her head and kissed his feet and anointed them with the ointment. 39 Now when the Pharisee who had invited him saw this, he said to himself, "If this man was a prophet, he would have known who and what sort of woman this is who is touching him, for she is a sinner." 40 And Jesus answering said to him, "Simon, I have something to say to you." And he answered, "Say it, Teacher."

41 "A certain moneylender had two debtors. One owed five hundred denarii, and the other fifty. 42 When they could not pay, he cancelled the debt of both. Now which of them will love him more?" 43 Simon answered, "The one, I suppose, for whom he cancelled the larger debt." And he said to him, "You have judged rightly." 44 Then turning toward the woman he said to Simon, "Do you see this woman? I entered your house; you gave me no water for my feet, but she has wet my feet with her tears and wiped them with her hair. 45 You gave me no kiss, but from the time I came in she has not ceased to kiss my feet. 46 You did not anoint my head with oil, but she has anointed my feet with ointment. 47 Therefore I tell you, her sins, which are many, are forgiven—for she loved much. But he who is forgiven little, loves little." 48 And he said to her, "Your sins are forgiven." 49 Then those who were at table with him began to say among themselves, "Who is this, who even forgives sins?" 50 And he said to the woman, "Your faith has saved you; go in peace." ESV

NOTE #1

Three other passages in the Gospels tell a similar story. The one in Luke is the only one that describes the woman as a sinner (probably a prostitute). The stories in Mark and Matthew occurred in the home of Simon the Leper, rather than in a Pharisee's home as reported in Luke. John's account occurred at the home of Lazarus, Martha, and Mary, with Mary being the woman who anoints Jesus with the oil (perfume). These other three passages are not the same event as the one reported in Luke. (See Mk 14:3-9; Mt 26:6-13; Jn 12:2-8.)

NOTE #2

Although there are several lessons and issues that might be raised in this passage, we will focus primarily on those related to the sinful woman.

The Context

There is nothing special about the context of this story. It occurs in the middle of several stories and parables that Luke relates about faith issues. It portrays Christ's mercy toward sinners in contrast to the self-centeredness of the Pharisees. The highlights of the story surrounding the sinful woman are:

- Jesus was invited to eat in the house of a Pharisee.

- A sinful woman ("prostitute") gained entry to the house.

- She wept and anointed Jesus' feet with her tears and fragrant oil (perfume).

- She wiped Jesus' feet with her hair while kissing His feet.

- The Pharisee host said to himself that Jesus should know this was a sinful woman if He were really a prophet.

- Jesus told a parable about two debtors.

- Jesus compared the woman's acts of worship and love to how Simon treated Him as a guest.

- Jesus said that her sins were forgiven, "for she loved much."

- Jesus told the woman, "Your faith has saved you."

What Do We Know?

We don't know for sure that the sinful woman was a prostitute but most commentaries agree that is a logical assumption. We do know she was described as a sinful woman, implying she was involved in some continual sin, most likely prostitution or adultery. The woman was clearly recognized by both Simon the Pharisee and Jesus as "a sinful woman." Her reputation seems commonly known and not in question.

A Pharisee would have avoided this woman because of her reputation and her sin. Yet Jesus made no attempt to shun the woman, and in fact, allowed her to touch Him, anoint Him, and wipe His feet with her hair.

The woman's hair was significant in this story. When a Jewish girl married, she put her hair up and would never thereafter appear in public with her hair down or unbound. It would have been very immodest for a woman to unbind her hair and still more shocking to use it to dry Jesus' feet.

It is interesting that the woman never spoke in this passage. It is possible that words were spoken, but Luke lets the woman do all her talking with her actions. And what her actions say is significant!

It's likely that the alabaster jar of oil (perfume) was the woman's most valuable possession. It might have been her ultimate hope to escape the prostitution trade. It is also likely that this perfume was used in her trade. The perfume was very valuable and yet she poured it all out on Jesus' feet. Some might suggest this act was a great waste while others consider it a dramatic act of worship.

The woman performed several gracious and loving acts at Jesus' feet: weeping, anointing Him with oil, kissing His feet, and wiping His feet with her hair. Why? The only hint we have of a motive is Jesus' comment after He told the Pharisee the parable: "That's why she loved much." Jesus related this love to forgiveness. Therefore, one explanation for her actions is that they were done out of love because she was forgiven. She was extremely grateful and showed her love through her actions. This suggests that the woman might have interacted with either Jesus or His disciples at a prior time.

Jesus contrasted the actions of the sinful woman to Simon's lack of hospitality. We do not know why Simon failed to provide normal acts of hospitality but he was found wanting as a host. Could he have wanted to put Jesus in an awkward position? Maybe! It is not clear if Simon was a bad host to all present or just to Jesus.

Implications and Observations

Given Jesus' criticism of Simon's hospitality, one might expect some kind of response from him, but the story ends without reporting any response. He might have been one of those at the table who said, "Who is this man who even forgives sins?" But other than this open-ended comment, we know of nothing that results from his interaction with Jesus.

The woman's actions were more than an act of worship. Not only was she openly worshipping her Savior but she invested a great deal of financial wealth, maybe her entire savings, in pouring her perfume on His feet! These seem to be the actions of a person who had heard of Jesus and been converted prior to coming to the house. It appears to be a planned act rather than a spontaneous event since she had intentionally brought the perfume with her. On the other hand, if this perfume was part of her trade she might have it with her wherever she went. It would not have been easy to work her way to the table to where Jesus was reclining, but once she got there, His reclining posture would have made it easy to anoint His feet.

Jews of that day did not associate with known sinners, so Jesus' response to her touch and actions would have grated against the customs and norms. Her actions, if not pure worship, were certainly an extravagant expression of devotion and gratitude for who He was and what He had done for her. Her tears would seem to be those of joy and gladness for the release she must have felt knowing that she was forgiven for the ugly work she had been performing.

The point of the parable was that someone who has been forgiven much responds with great love and gratitude, while someone who has been forgiven less will respond with less. This woman realized she was a sinner and needed forgiveness to be right with God. The woman expressed her great love toward Jesus through these acts of worship because she had been forgiven much.

But why was she really there in the Pharisee's house. Allow me [the author] to provide a few personal thoughts. I believe that the prostitute could have already repented and been forgiven at a previous time either by Jesus or one of the Apostles. After realizing the huge burden that had been lifted from her shoulders and hearing that Jesus was nearby in the home of one of the Pharisees, she wanted to demonstrate her great love and gratitude. What could she do? She saw the alabaster jar and immediately formed a plan. The perfume represented her trade as a prostitute. She used this with the men she was with and the amount in the jar likely represented her accumulated life as a "sinful woman." What better act of gratitude and release than to dispose of it by anointing Jesus' feet? The woman used her most treasured possession (the perfume) to proclaim her statement or commitment of faith. Words were unnecessary!

Discussion Questions

A. GENERAL

A1. Where was Jesus and why?

A2. What problems would Simon, the Pharisee, have because of the woman's profession?

A3. If <u>you</u> were Simon and you knew who the woman was and you observed her enter the house, what would <u>you</u> have done?

A4. List all the significant actions the woman took. Which one do you think <u>most</u> represented her commitment or attitude?

A5. Why didn't the woman anoint Jesus' head with the perfume, which would have been more customary?

A6. The text doesn't say why the woman was weeping. What do you think was the reason?

A7. Do you think the woman intentionally wet Jesus' feet or was it an accident because she was at His feet? Why?

A8. How would you contrast the woman's actions (in A4 above) with those of the Pharisee (Simon)?

A9. Contrast how Simon and the woman thought of themselves.

A10. Is there anything meaningful about the fact that the woman wiped Jesus' feet with her hair rather than some portion of her clothing?

A11. Do you think you would have done what the woman did? Why? Why not?

A12. The perfume was very valuable. It may have been the woman's only possession of value. How would you describe the perfume and what it represented or expressed?

A13. How would you contrast Jesus' attitudes toward Simon, a Pharisee, and the woman who is supposedly a prostitute? Explain.

A14. How should Simon have responded to the parable and Jesus' act of forgiving the woman's sins?

A15. What are some questions Simon might have asked to gain understanding of Jesus' actions?

A16. How do you react personally to this act of worship by the sinful woman?

A17. If all you knew about the woman in this passage was contained in verse 38, what words or phrases would you use to describe her?

A18. The woman would normally have been shunned by the Pharisees (and others) because of her sinful past. Do we treat people like this today? If so, who are they and why do we treat them as lepers in the church?

A19. Put into words what you think Jesus' response to the sinful woman <u>meant to her</u>.

48 . . . "Your sins are forgiven." 49 Then those who were at table with him began to say among themselves, "Who is this, who even forgives sins?" 50 And he said to the woman, "Your faith has saved you; go in peace." ESV

Q. Although the woman seemed to be overwhelmed with love for her Savior, what is it that Jesus said saved her?

A20. All Simon saw was a sinful woman, but Jesus saw something else. If you had been there, what would you have seen? Why?

A21. It could not have been accidental that Simon ignored all the normal actions of a host. Why do you think Simon intentionally ignored Jesus?

A22. God loves people who take spiritual risks. Jesus confirmed this woman's forgiveness and gave her a new lease on life. She was not asked to invest her wealth in an act of worship, but she did. Can you think of any other stories or situations in Scripture where someone took a big spiritual risk? Explain.

A23. Can you think of other acts of worship in Scripture that are as meaningful as what this woman did?

B. APPLICATION

B1. This woman was so overwhelmed with gratitude that she ignored social norms. She was totally committed to Christ. What would have to happen in your life today to give your savings (or most of it) to a Kingdom cause and completely trust in God?

B2. Do your actions speak for you? Would your actions convict you of being a Christ-follower?

B3. Do you need to do something <u>bold</u> for Christ?

B4. Do you need to imitate this woman in any way?

The Potter
and the clay

Occurrences of "potter" or "potters" in Bible: 18
There are multiple and different references to "the potter"
spread throughout Scripture. Five occur in the best known
reference in the Parable of the Potter (Jeremiah 18:1-6) and
several others are related to this parable.

Themes: God's Sovereignty; Sanctification

Scripture

Parable of the Potter
Jeremiah 18:1-6   *The word that came to Jeremiah from the Lord:*
2 "Arise, and go down to the potter's house, and there I will let you
hear my words." 3 So I went down to the potter's house, and there
he was working at his wheel. 4 And the vessel he was making of
clay was spoiled in the potter's hand, and he reworked it into
another vessel, as it seemed good to the potter to do. 5 Then the
word of the Lord came to me: 6 "O house of Israel, can I not do with
you as this potter has done, declares the Lord. Behold, like the clay
in the potter's hand, so are you in my hand, O house of Israel. ESV

God The Potter
Romans 9:19-21   *You will say to me then, "Why does he still find*
fault? For who can resist his will?" 20 But who are you, O man, to
answer back to God? Will what is molded say to its molder, "Why
have you made me like this?" 21 Has the potter no right over the
clay, to make out of the same lump one vessel for honored use and
another for dishonorable use? ESV

The Context

The parable or story about the potter and the potter's house appears in Jeremiah in the midst of warnings and exhortations to Judah regarding her pending destruction. The northern kingdom of Israel had already been exiled because of her sin and rebellion, but that lesson had not been enough to keep the southern kingdom of Judah from the same fate. God continued to send prophets to warn the people about their behavior but the warnings fell on deaf ears.

God called Jeremiah to proclaim His judgment on the people. These warnings occur in chapters 2-35 of the book of Jeremiah, and in the middle of the warnings God told Jeremiah to go down to the potter's house where He would give Jeremiah a message for the people of Judah.

What Do We Know?

When Jeremiah reached the potter's house, the potter was working at his wheel and the clay he was using was marred or damaged. Because something was wrong with the clay, the pot was not turning out as desired. The potter decided not to proceed with the imperfect pot. Rather, he formed a new pot from the clay to be used according to what he thought was best. For example, the initial pot may have been a large water jug and the second a small pitcher.

God then gave Jeremiah a prophetic message: Because the Lord is the God of Israel, He would treat Judah just like the potter treated the clay. Just as the potter had total control over what he made on the wheel, so God would exercise His sovereign hand over Judah. In

Jeremiah 18:11 God told Jeremiah exactly what to tell the people in Judah and Jerusalem:

> ***God is preparing a disaster against you,***
> ***so repent from your evil ways!***

Implications and Observations

Although the message is quite clear and should be easily understood, the people did not have ears to hear. They were so wrapped up in unrighteousness, injustice, and unfaithfulness that they simply ignored Jeremiah, as they had ignored previous prophets God had sent to warn them.

Jeremiah used the illustration of the potter to help the people understand that God was sovereign and that He would not hesitate to start over with His clay if it could not or would not result in what He wanted to produce. If the clay had impurities, the potter would take it off the wheel, smash it and rework it until all the impurities were removed and it could be used again. The clay was not discarded, but was made into another vessel that would better serve the potter's purposes and plans.

Isaiah had used references to a potter 60 to 80 years prior to Jeremiah's prophecy:

> Isaiah 45:9; 64:8
> 45:9 *"Woe to him who strives with him who formed him, a pot among earthen pots! Does the clay say to him who forms it, 'What are you making?' or 'Your work has no handles'"? . . . 64:8 But now, O Lord, you are our Father; we are the clay, and you are our potter; we are all the work of your hand.* ESV

Although God had serious words for Judah, the people refused to listen:

> Jeremiah 18:12   *But they say, "That is in vain! We will follow our own plans, and will every one act according to the stubbornness of his evil heart."* ESV

Ten Principles of the Potter and the Clay[1]

This study will not examine the text as closely as we have in our other investigations of obscure characters. The basic story of the potter is relatively easy to understand – God is sovereign and man must never think that he (the clay) has the power or ability to determine his own destiny. God is and will always be in charge!

In this lesson we will examine how the nature and relationship of God and man are much like the relationship of the potter and the clay.

A. SOURCE: Man and clay both come from the earth.

The potter cannot use just any kind of material to make pottery. He needs good clay from the ground. The potter digs clay with a plan in mind – he wants to make a pot. He must prepare the clay before he can begin making anything. It must be softened and worked into a pliable state so that its inherent hardness can be formed into the desired end result. The potter will pound, beat, or knead the clay until it is ready for the wheel.

A1. What did God do in Genesis 1 that relates to what the potter does before he begins to work?

A2. What else did God do in Genesis 2:7 to make man alive that relates to the potter?

B. NATURE: Man is inherently sinful and clay is innately impure.

With Adam's fall, man acquired sin and evil and was no longer pure and righteous. We have evil tendencies, weaknesses, and harmful behaviors that God must remove from our makeup. Just as clay contains impurities that must be removed in order for the potter to make a good pot, so man's sinful nature must be overcome. The good news for man is that an all-powerful, all-knowing God is shaping and forming our lives into the unique form and image that will suit His purposes.

B1. In this story of the potter, the clay or pot that is marred is not discarded. How would you compare this with how God relates to man?

B2. After a pot is initially formed, it is put in a kiln and fired to 1000-1500C. How would you compare this final process for a pot to what God does with man?

C. PROCESS: There are procedures and techniques necessary to form both the clay and man.

Webster defines "form" as follows: "to get, create, or develop something over a period of time; to arrange in order." The potter forms the pot with techniques and skills that when used properly will produce a finished product that is appropriate for the potter's intended use.

Depending on the nature and purpose of the pot, the potter uses different techniques to form, mold, shape, and create the final vessel. God also uses different techniques to form us into the people He wants us to be. The potter controls the speed of the wheel as he forms a pot. God also controls the speed and timeframe as He develops His people.

Genesis 2:7 *then the Lord God formed the man of dust from the ground and breathed into his nostrils the breath of life, and the man became a living creature. ESV*

      C1. What are some techniques God uses to form and shape His people?

      C2. Which of these techniques has God used in your life?

D. REQUIRED INGREDIENTS: The potter needs water and God requires the Word.

The potter must add water to the clay in order to make it pliable enough to be shaped and molded. If too little water is added the clay remains hard and rigid, and it cannot be used on the wheel. God uses His Word to wash us clean from the sinful nature that controls our flesh. He needs to instill the truth and teach us righteousness. Just as man cannot survive without water, the potter needs water to form and work the clay. Just as water is a necessary ingredient so is the Word of God as it feeds, restores, and sanctifies man's heart.

The potter applies the water constantly as he works with the clay. He cannot use the clay until there is enough water in the mixture and he adds more water with his hands as he manipulates the clay. Neither can God begin the sanctification process until the Word has begun to take hold in our lives. But it does not stop with one dose! God continues to teach, grow, and mature us through the knowledge and application of His Word in our lives.

> Ephesians 5:26   *that he might sanctify her, having cleansed her by the washing of water with the word.* ESV

D1. What do you think happens if too little water is used in the clay? How might you relate this to the amount of God's Word necessary for man?

D2. Must a non-believer begin reading and studying the Bible before he can be saved? Why? Why not?

D3. If a saved believer does not read the Bible, what happens? What are some of the likely scenarios?

E. ORIENTATION: The clay must be centered on the wheel and man must be focused on Jesus.

When the clay is ready the potter places it on the wheel in the exact center. If the lump of clay is centered, the clay will spin properly and the potter can begin to form and work the clay. If the clay is not centered on the wheel, disaster is likely because the potter will not be able to work the clay properly. The vessel will break apart and may even fly off the wheel.

Just as the clay must be centered on the wheel, so must man be centered on Jesus. If we have not put Christ in our lives, God will not begin to work or be present in our lives. If we have not made Jesus the center and focus of our life, little growth will happen. Jesus must be both Savior and Lord. If Christ is not Lord, then He is not the one we are looking to for truth and guidance. If the lord of our life is wealth, power, sex, sports, drugs, or any other secular value, we will not grow in our faith.

Just as a clay pot will fall apart on the spinning wheel if it is not centered, our lives will fall apart if we are not centered on Jesus. This is confirmed in Psalm 127:1, "*Unless the Lord builds the house, those who build it labor in vain. . .*" ESV

> E1. What do you believe is the biggest stumbling block (human characteristic) to being fully committed to Christ?

> E2. What does it mean to <u>you</u> that Jesus is Lord of your life?

E3. Write a short sentence explaining what it means for your life to be _centered_ on Jesus.

F. PATIENCE: The forming and molding process takes time.

Forming a pot and sanctifying believers are both evolving processes. The clay does not instantly turn into a finished pot, just as the believer does not instantly become mature and totally committed to Christ. Both processes take time. The ideal speed for the pot is slow and steady. The potter can set the speed of the wheel at any speed but if it goes too fast the clay will either tear or come apart on the wheel. The potter sets the speed of the wheel to turn at a steady rate that will give him time to form and mold the clay as he desires.

F1. How would you relate this characteristic of the potter's process to God and man?

F2. What characteristics and values of the secular world work against slow and steady growth?

G. PURPOSE: God will develop man to his full potential.

The lump of clay will start to grow taller as the potter works the clay and it continues to spin on the wheel. Unfortunately in life when we get to this point we often think we have arrived. We get satisfied when we are only half finished. It can be the same way in our spiritual life. We need to continually press on and allow God to take us as far as He wants us go. It is a tragic waste of potential if we become complacent and stop growing as God guides us to spiritual maturity. We need to press on to reach our potential and the goal He has for our lives.

G1. Are you fully utilizing your secular skills and spiritual gifts for the work of the Kingdom?

G2. What does God want you to do? What is God calling you to do? What are you good at?

G3. If you feel that you are not fully engaged with God or the church, what will it take for you to allow God to finish the work He started?

H. EXCESS CLAY: God will always be doing pruning in your life.

Eventually the potter will take a knife and cut off any excess clay that has accumulated around the pot as he molded, scraped, and shaped it. The potter will cut off the excess and smooth the rough edges so the pot turns out complete and beautiful to the eye.

In the same way, God will always be cutting away qualities that He does not want in your life. God may remove some of your friends because of the negative influence they have on you and your spiritual development. He may move you to a new city or a new job. Though this cutting away can be very painful, it is always for your ultimate good. You will be much better off cooperating with the Lord when He begins cutting away negative characteristics from your life and personality.

> H1. What has God already cut from your life? What might God want to cut out of your life or personality in the future?

> H2. How about your life priorities? Are they aligned with God?

>> Q. Do you have life priorities?

>> - Is your job more important than your relationship with Christ?
>> - Do you put family ahead of Christ?
>> - Do you have hobbies or activities that are more important than Christ?

I. FOCUS: God's attention is always on you.

Once the potter begins to work the clay, he never looks away from it until he is finished. If he takes his eyes and attention off the pot as he shapes and molds it, he could make a big mistake and destroy his work. In the same way, once we come into a true relationship with God, He will never take His eyes and attention off us. We can fully trust God to complete the work that He has begun.

> Philippians 1:6   *And I am sure of this, that he who began a good work in you will bring it to completion at the day of Jesus Christ.* ESV

Just as the clay does not fight against the hands of the potter, we should not fight against the hands of God when He is working in our lives. Just as the clay cannot mold itself, man cannot produce the result God has planned for each of us. We are each special and unique in the eyes of God. His focus is on us and our relationship with Him. Just as the vessel in the hands of the potter will have a special use and purpose, so will the person who allows God to shape and mold him into a child of God.

I1. Did you ever fight against the hand of God in your life? What happened?

I2. Do you have a friend or family member who needs to hear these ten principles?

J. WARNING: The vessel is fragile.

Clay pots are quite easily cracked or broken. One must be careful and protective. Sometimes the potter can repair the vessel. Sometimes he cannot.

> Jeremiah 19:11   *and shall say to them, "Thus says the Lord of hosts: So will I break this people and this city, as one breaks a potter's vessel, so that it can never be mended. . ."* ESV

If a vessel is damaged during the molding process, it can be repaired or remolded. If the damage occurs after the vessel has been fired it is irreparable. The pot can be glued back together, but it will never be the same.

> J1. What does the firing process do to the pot?

> J2. What do you think God might do to harden (finish) a disciple for His ultimate use?

K. WILL: The will of the Potter.

After the potter has worked the clay into a pliable state, placed the mound of clay on the wheel, centered it, and added the right amount of water, he is ready to form the clay into the desired vessel. The potter knows in advance what he wants the result to be – he does not start forming and working the clay until everything is ready and he has a finished vessel in mind. It is the potter's will that determines the outcome and result of the work he performs.

The potter's hands work on both the inside and outside of the clay to mold, shape, and transform it into the desired result. His hands often go deep down into the clay to push the material in the middle of the mound to the outer edges. It is impossible to make a pot unless the hands of the potter are inside the vessel molding it and nudging it outward.

God does the same thing in sanctifying and purifying His people. Our lives cannot be shaped and formed by surface scraping. The inner being must be sanctified, which requires significant work on our inner nature. This is not always a pleasant experience. Forming can be painful. Man loves the flesh. Worldly lusts and values are difficult to remove when everything around us is at odds with the work God is doing in our hearts. The removal process may take a long time and may produce suffering and heartache. But God knows what He wants the end result to be, because just like the potter, He started with a plan and purpose in mind.

Sin is never easy to stop or remove. It is often acceptable to the world. Pride and arrogance will often cause delays and loss of progress, but God is faithful. His will cannot be compromised. He wants the very best from what He has formed from the dust of the earth! God and the potter both know exactly what they want the result to be. They know exactly what kind of vessel will result from the molding and the pressure they apply to the clay.

If you were asked the question, "What is God doing in your life?" how would you respond? When we are not expecting this question, it may be difficult to know what to say. Upon reflection, we might respond, "Why would God be working in my life at all?" and, secondly, "What would be the nature of what He is doing?"

God would be doing something in my life for three reasons:

       a) to change <u>me</u>,

       b) to impact <u>others</u> through me, or

       c) to improve the relationship between <u>Him</u> and me.

So, what's the Potter doing in your life these days?

Ananias & Sapphira
they dropped dead

Occurrences of "Ananias" in the Bible: 3
Occurrences of "Sapphira" in the Bible: 1

Themes: Integrity; Pride; Consequences

Scripture

Acts 5:1-11
But a man named Ananias, with his wife Sapphira, sold a piece of property, 2 and with his wife's knowledge he kept back for himself some of the proceeds and brought only a part of it and laid it at the apostles' feet. 3 But Peter said, "Ananias, why has Satan filled your heart to lie to the Holy Spirit and to keep back for yourself part of the proceeds of the land? 4 While it remained unsold, did it not remain your own? And after it was sold, was it not at your disposal? Why is it that you have contrived this deed in your heart? You have not lied to men but to God." 5 When Ananias heard these words, he fell down and breathed his last. And great fear came upon all who heard of it. 6 The young men rose and wrapped him up and carried him out and buried him.

7 After an interval of about three hours his wife came in, not knowing what had happened. 8 And Peter said to her, "Tell me whether you sold the land for so much." And she said, "Yes, for so much." 9 But Peter said to her, "How is it that you have agreed together to test the Spirit of the Lord? Behold, the feet of those who have buried your husband are at the door, and they will carry you out." 10 Immediately she fell down at his feet and breathed her last. When the young men came in they found her dead, and they

43

carried her out and buried her beside her husband. 11 And great fear came upon the whole church and upon all who heard of these things. ESV

The Context

This event involving Ananias and his wife Sapphire occurred very soon after Pentecost, in the early days of the church. Because of the very unique circumstances that existed at that time, the church was living in a communal environment:

> Acts 2:44-45   *And all who believed were together and had all things in common. 45 And they were selling their possessions and belongings and distributing the proceeds to all, as any had need.* ESV

There were no needy people among the group because as needs arose, people sold land or property and gave the proceeds to the Apostles to share with those in need. One such person was Barnabas, who sold a field and brought the money to the Apostles (Acts 4:36-37).

What Do We Know?

Following Barnabas' generosity, Scripture reports that Ananias and Sapphira also sold some property, but apparently they "kept back" some of the proceeds. The Greek word for "kept back" can also be translated "embezzled." The author says that Ananias did this with his wife's knowledge.

Peter first confronted Ananias about the shortfall. We are not told how Peter knew about the money being kept back. Peter asked Ananias why he did this and Ananias immediately dropped dead without responding. Some of the young men got up immediately and took the body to be buried.

After three hours passed, Ananias' wife Sapphira returned without knowing that her husband had died. Peter did not tell her that

Ananias was dead, but asked her to confirm the price of the sale. She also lied about the proceeds and dropped dead like Ananias, just as the young men who buried him returned.

> Acts 5:11   *And great fear came upon the whole church and upon all who heard of these things.* ESV

Implications and Observations

There is a similar story about a thief named Achan in Joshua 7:19-26. These two stories have some striking similarities even though the events are separated by hundreds of years:

1) Both stories involved insiders who were part of the religious community.

2) Both kept back something they were obligated not to keep and lied about the circumstances. For Achan it was the spoils of war and for Ananias it was the proceeds from the sale of property.

3) Both Ananias and Achan acted intentionally, not through accident or misunderstanding. They knew what they were doing and intended to receive personal gain.

4) Both demonstrated little concern for the spiritual community and the impact of their actions on the community. Achan caused God to withdraw His assistance to Israel in battle which resulted in loss of life. Ananias lied to God, establishing a dangerous precedent for the communal fellowship and potentially losing God's favor.

5) Both situations prompted God's intervention. God exposed Achan to Joshua through a selection process, and in Acts, God exacted a deadly punishment upon Ananias and Sapphira.

6) Both were found guilty and executed in an unusual manner.

7) Both events were dramatic warnings to others in the community or church.

A significant difference between Achan and Ananias is that Achan's sin was pure thievery; he simply took spoils that were devoted to the Lord. Ananias kept back funds intended for needy people in the church. There was absolutely no reason for Ananias to promise the money and then hold some back since he and Sapphira were not actually obligated to give any of the money to anybody.

Sin can damage the integrity of an entire church. The biggest damage is usually caused when a leader is publically exposed because of some sin he or she committed. It is usually a serious sin like embezzlement, sexual immorality, addiction, or the like.

This was first a message to the church, and based on 5:11 the church got the message. But 5:11 also says that everyone who heard the story was impacted ("great fear").

To have "great fear" come upon the unbelieving community because God demonstrated His power and truth in the church can be both a good and bad thing. People are open to the Gospel in times of persecution, oppression, suffering, and supernatural events. We know that the people were already impressed by the healing miracles the apostles were performing. With this event they heard of judgment carried out on a family who lied to an all-powerful God. The impact could be life-changing.

One might assume that this would have hurt the church. But I think it could have also been extremely appealing to men and women who wanted to live under a mighty and holy God. It is probably fair to assume that this situation did not cause great numbers to flock to the church, because most outsiders would not understand what and why all this happened. Some hearing this would assume the worst, and want nothing to do with the church. However, those who gave serious thought might recognize the power and integrity of this Jesus whom the Christians followed. Jesus was nothing like the hypocritical Sadducees and Pharisees.

One last interesting fact is that they buried the bodies immediately. Normally in Jewish culture bodies would be buried within 24 hours but here it appears that the body was not even prepared in any way for burial. This type of treatment would normally be reserved for only the vilest of criminals.

Discussion Questions

A. GENERAL

A1. Has anyone present ever told a:

> a. Little white lie?
> b. Bold-face lie?

> Q. So, why aren't we all dead?

A2. What do you think this story is really about? What is one word or phrase that represents the foundational issue in this story? Explain.

A3. What would you name as the primary sin underlying Ananias and Sapphira's behavior? Why?

A4. What do you suspect could be some of the practical reasons Ananias and Sapphira lied about the money?

A5. What does 5:4 say about Ananias' need to deceive? Can you put this is your own language to clarify what Peter was saying?

A6. How do you think Peter knew about Ananias keeping money back?

A7. What did God accomplish with this act of judgment? Why do you think God dealt so severely with Ananias and Sapphira?

A8. Do you find it strange that Sapphira was not told immediately about her husband's death when she approached the house?

A9. Was their punishment fair and just?

A10. It appears they agreed to be very generous, but then simply were not as generous as they had promised. Does that warrant God's wrath?

A11. How would you have felt if you had just finished burying Ananias and returned to find out that you must now bury Sapphira?

A12. What exactly did Peter accuse Ananias of doing and why?

Q. What do you think all this means specifically? What must have occurred for Peter to make this accusation?

A13. Why was Sapphira accused of testing the Spirit of the Lord. What do you think that means?

A14. What is the significance of 5:5 and 5:11 . . . "*Great fear came on the whole church?*"

Q. Was this "fear" good or bad?

A15. Why did God choose to act in this way? Why didn't He render this type of just punishment in all the other life situations where it was equally deserved? You and I have probably done things equally as bad and the result was not instant death. Why?

A16. Why would God want this story in the Bible? At first glance this does not seem to be a situation that would impress outsiders or seekers. Why not leave this story out altogether? If it were your choice, would you put it in the Bible or leave it out? Why?

A17. How do outsiders typically evaluate the integrity or trustworthiness of a particular church?

Q. Why is corrupting church members a favorite tactic of Satan today?

A18. Today if a Christian leader speaks out nationally against a particular sin, what typically happens? Why?

Q. What might be an alternate strategy to calling out a nation or group, or a particular sinful act?

B. APPLICATION

B1. Has someone's generosity ever inspired you to act generously? Explain.

B2. In what ways do we lie to each other in our Christian communities and small groups?

B3. Have you ever tried to nudge or influence God? Maybe you pray frequently for wants rather than needs. Or maybe you are openly "testing" God and thinking He doesn't know or care. How did that work out for you?

B4. Are you in any danger of punishment? Or are consequences surely coming, and you just don't know what and when?

Jabez
he prayed for blessing

Occurrences of "Jabez" in the Bible: 3

Themes: Prayer

Scripture

1 Chronicles 4:9-10   ESV
Jabez was more honorable than his brothers; and his mother called his name Jabez, saying, "Because I bore him in pain." 10 Jabez called upon the God of Israel, saying, "Oh that you would bless me and enlarge my border, and that your hand might be with me, and that you would keep me from harm so that it might not bring me pain!" And God granted what he asked.

1 Chronicles 4:9-10   HCSB
Jabez was more honorable than his brothers. His mother named him Jabez and said, "I gave birth to him in pain." 10 Jabez called out to the God of Israel: "If only You would bless me, extend my border, let Your hand be with me, and keep me from harm, so that I will not cause any pain." And God granted his request.

1 Chronicles 4:9-10   NKJV
Now Jabez was more honorable than his brothers, and his mother called his name Jabez, saying, "Because I bore him in pain." 10 And Jabez called on the God of Israel saying, "Oh, that You would bless me indeed, and enlarge my territory, that Your hand would be with me, and that You would keep me from evil, that I may not cause pain!" So God granted him what he requested.

NOTE: Some translations translate, "*so that it might not bring me pain*"(ESV) as a request not to cause pain to someone else. Both interpretations are reasonable given the original text, but they provide different perspectives. The HCSB and NKJV above provide this latter interpretation in comparison with the ESV.

The Context

This passage occurs in the middle of a series of genealogies describing the ancestry of the Hebrew nation. Chapters 1 and 2 trace the Israelites history from Adam through Caleb's sons. Chapter 3 describes David's descendants, and Chapter 4 lists other descendants of Judah. It's here that we find Jabez. In general, no information is given other than the names linked to the parents. However, occasionally a little more detail is provided, and this is how we learn more about Jabez. This is the only place in the Bible Jabez or his prayer is mentioned.

What Do We Know?

The passage says that Jabez was more honorable than his brothers, but it does not explain what that means. It also tells us that he was birthed in pain but there is no explanation of that statement either.

We are told of a prayer Jabez prayed:

- He asked to be blessed.
- He asked that his border [or *territory*] be enlarged meaning an increase of his wealth and influence.
- He asked that God's hand to be upon him, that is, God's protection and empowerment.
- He asked that he would be protected from harm and pain, or that he would not cause pain.

Lastly, and perhaps most importantly, we are told that God granted his requests. These are very straightforward requests. One might think that asking for blessing is presumptuous, but apparently God found it acceptable as the text tells us He granted the request. Jabez's first request, "bless me," is very general. It is reasonable to look at the remainder of the requests as specific ways in which he wishes to be blessed.

Implications and Observations

First and foremost in making any observations about this prayer and its implications, we should remember that God answered the prayer. Therefore, we must assume that the prayer was acceptable and appropriate.

Given the fact that God granted Jabez's requests, what might we assume about those requests? First, blessings are available and God will grant them. Second, wealth and power are not inherently bad, and God is willing to grant them to those He chooses. Third, He will empower us in some or in many areas of our lives, but we may need to ask. Fourth, pain and evil are real and we need protection from it.

Finally, we need to pray with the right motives. Jabez did not wish to be harmed or cause harm that might result in pain in his life or the life of another. Having the right motive is also confirmed in the New Testament:

> James 4:3   *You ask and do not receive, because you ask wrongly, to spend it on your passions.* ESV

We have two hints in this passage as to why God might have chosen to answer this prayer:

- Jabez was more honorable than his brothers, and
- He asked God to prevent him from causing pain (HCSB and NKJV).

If the HCSB and NKJV translations are closer to the correct understanding, we observe a humble spirit in Jabez in his desire not to cause pain to others. Obviously God knows Jabez's heart and in the end, that may determine whether God is going to answer a prayer of this magnitude.

Discussion Questions

A. GENERAL

A1. Why would the author include this extra information about Jabez? What makes his prayer worthy of mention?

A2. What do you think it means that Jebez was "more honorable than his brothers"?

A3. List other prayers the Bible tells us God answered.

A4. After God answered this prayer, what other requests might Jabez need or want to pray? For each of his requests, how might Jabez expand his prayer to ensure a desired result?

- Be blessed.

- Increase territory.

- Protection and empowerment

- Protected from harm or evil.

- Not cause pain.

A5. How can we pray this prayer and not be selfish? What is our motive?

B. BORDER (Territory)

B1. Territory (land) was a fundamental wealth component during the time of Jabez. If you were praying a similar prayer today, what might you pray for? Why?

B2. What other areas of life (other than wealth or influence) could you ask to be expanded?

Q. In which one of these areas could you personally have the biggest impact? Why?

B3. Is it appropriate to pray for wealth?

B4. If "territory" represents relationships, in what ways do you think God might want you to enlarge your personal territory? Why?

C. BLESSING

C1. Jabez's first request was to be blessed. Do you think it is appropriate to ask God to bless you?

C2. When <u>you</u> ask for blessing what are <u>you</u> personally thinking you are asking for? What are you expecting?

C3. How do you think God responds to an "open-ended" honest request for blessing? (An open-ended request means there are no specifics.)

C4. What would your life look like if God poured out His blessing on you and your family? In what areas of your life would He be most likely to bless you? Why?

C5. Do you think God's blessings are conditional or unconditional? Why? Why not?

D. POWER

D1. Was there a time in <u>your</u> life when you asked for God's power? What happened?

D2. What are some of the excuses we all give for staying in our comfort zones?

E. EVIL

E1. What evil do you want God to protect you from? Are there areas of your life that you play close to the edge where you would desire God's power to keep you safe?

E2. If Satan designed a trap or temptation to snare you, what would it be? Or what is your greatest weakness? We are normally vulnerable at our weak points.

F. APPLICATION

F1. What, if anything, are you doing today that requires God's power, other than life in general?

F2. Do you have not because you ask not? Does your prayer life need to improve and become more focused?

F3. Are you asking for the things you need or for what you want?

F4. Do your prayers have eternal significance? For example, do you pray:

> That my life would bring praise and honor to God.
> That I would know God.
> That I have a right relationship with Christ.
> That my worship is acceptable and heartfelt.
> That I thirst for the truth of God's Word.
> That I love God with all my heart, strength, mind, soul.
> That Christ is the central focus and reality of my life.
> That I always have a thankful heart.

F5. Are your prayers big enough?

Challenge Exercise:

Expand each section of Jabez's prayer. Rewrite the prayer so that it is personal, in modern terms, and adds substance to your request. I have expanded the first request. Do at least one of the others for yourself.

"Bless Me"

Lord, I desire Your blessing! Please pour out in my life every possible blessing You desire for me. Father, I want You working in my life and I need the guidance and direction of the Holy Spirit so that my walk is pleasing to You. Bless me so that I can be a blessing to others. I desire Your blessing so that You receive honor and thanksgiving from others who see You working in my life. Bless me O Lord. AMEN.

Q. When you read the above what strikes you? What do you notice about this prayer?

Expanded Prayer

Subject: _____

Prayer: _____

_____

_____

_____

_____

_____

_____

_____

_____

_____

Zophar
one of Job's friends

Occurrences of "Zophar" in the Bible: 4

Themes: Hope

NOTE: The word "hope" occurs 167 times in the Bible. It is Used 18 times in the Book of Job, more than in any other book, except Psalms. In seventy-five percent of the Psalms passages, the reference is to hope in God or His word.

Scripture

Job 11 Zophar Speaks: You Deserve Worse

Then Zophar the Naamathite answered and said: 2 "Should a multitude of words go unanswered, and a man full of talk be judged right? 3 Should your babble silence men, and when you mock, shall no one shame you? 4 For you say, 'My doctrine is pure, and I am clean in God's eyes.' 5 But oh, that God would speak and open his lips to you, 6 and that he would tell you the secrets of wisdom! For he is manifold in understanding. Know then that God exacts of you less than your guilt deserves.

7 "Can you find out the deep things of God? Can you find out the limit of the Almighty? 8 It is higher than heaven—what can you do? Deeper than Sheol—what can you know? 9 Its measure is longer than the earth and broader than the sea. 10 If he passes through and imprisons and summons the court, who can turn him back? 11 For he knows worthless men; when he sees iniquity, will he not consider it? 12 But a stupid man will get understanding when a wild donkey's colt is born a man!

13 "If you prepare your heart, you will stretch out your hands toward him. 14 If iniquity is in your hand, put it far away, and let not injustice dwell in your tents. 15 Surely then you will lift up your face without blemish; you will be secure and will not fear. 16 You will forget your misery; you will remember it as waters that have passed away. 17 And your life will be brighter than the noonday; its darkness will be like the morning. 18 And you will feel secure, because there is hope; you will look around and take your rest in security. 19 You will lie down, and none will make you afraid; many will court your favor. 20 But the eyes of the wicked will fail; all way of escape will be lost to them, and their hope is to breathe their last." ESV

The Context

Job was under attack by Satan:

- His oxen and donkeys were stolen and his servants were killed (Job 1:12-15).
- His sheep were killed along with the servant caretakers (Job 1:16).
- His camels were stolen and their servant caretakers killed (Job 1:17).
- His children were killed when his house collapsed (Job 1:18-19).

Job's troubles did not end there. He was afflicted with painful sores all over his body. But in all this *Job did not sin* in what he said (2:10).

Job 2:11-13   Job's Three Friends

Now when Job's three friends heard of all this evil that had come upon him, they came each from his own place, Eliphaz the Temanite, Bildad the Shuhite, and Zophar the Naamathite. They made an appointment together to come to show him sympathy and comfort him. 12 And when they saw him from a distance, they did not recognize him. And they raised their voices and wept, and they tore their robes and sprinkled dust on their heads toward heaven. 13 And they sat with him on the ground seven days and seven nights, and no one spoke a word to him, for they saw that his suffering was very great. ESV

Zophar accused Job of wickedness and hypocrisy, urging him to repent. He suggested that God was being very gracious in forgetting some of Job's sin (Job 11:6). He openly accused Job of sin and in 11:13-15 made it clear that he believed all of Job's problems were the result of his sin. He suggested that all Job had to do to get back in God's good graces was to repent.

Zophar's first speech climaxed in the last four verses (17-20) when he told Job there was hope. Bildad, the second of Job's friends (chapter 8) ended his first speech in a similar manner. He did not use the word hope, but he described it: *"Behold, God will not reject a blameless man, nor take the hand of evildoers. 21 He will yet fill your mouth with laughter, and your lips with shouting. 22 Those who hate you will be clothed with shame, and the tent of the wicked will be no more."* (Job 8:20-22 ESV)

Thus, Bildad also gave Job reason to hope.

What Do We Know?

A close reading of the speeches delivered by Job's friends reveals that although their hearts were in the right place, their theology was a bit twisted. They came to sympathize with Job and give him hope (2:11-13). How else can you explain three men sitting on the ground for seven days, saying nothing? They were there to bring hope and comfort to Job.

In their first speeches, all three men mention "hope" and gave Job encouraging words, along with some counsel that was not particularly on target, primarily because they did not know the whole story. They also believed in the erroneous theology that all suffering was the result of sin and if Job stopped sinning, his troubles would go away.

The focus of this study is on what Zophar and his two friends intended to do: bring hope! What is hope? How important is hope and where does it come from? What does the Bible tell us about hope?

Definitions:

MERRIAM-WEBSTER: (1) anticipating something good happening; (2) to desire with the expectation of obtaining; (3) to expect with confidence; (4) the expectation of success.

BIBLICAL: In the Bible, the word hope stands for both the act of hoping (Rom 4:18; 1 Cor 9:10) and the thing hoped for (Col 1:5; 1 Peter 1:3). Hope does not arise from the individual's desires or wishes but from God, who is Himself the believer's hope. Genuine biblical hope is not wishful thinking, but a firm assurance of things that are unseen and still in the future (Rom 8:24-25; Heb 11:1, 7).[2]

CONCLUSION: Hope is *confident expectancy*.

Hope vs. Faith

There can be some confusion about how the Bible uses "faith" and "hope." In my opinion there are many instances when the two words could be interchanged and the meaning would not change. Technically there is a difference and a theologian could argue that difference. We will not do that because it is not important to the focus of this study. The definition of faith found in Hebrews 11:1 actually includes the word hope: "*Now faith is the assurance of things hoped for, the conviction of things not seen.*" ESV

Although the goal or objective of our Biblical hope is certain, we have not yet attained it, therefore, in that sense it is a reality that will occur in the future.

> Romans 8:23-25   *And not only the creation, but we ourselves, who have the firstfruits of the Spirit, groan inwardly as we wait eagerly for adoption as sons, the redemption of our bodies. 24 For in this hope we were saved. Now hope that is seen is not hope. For who hopes for what he sees? 25 But if we hope for what we do not see, we wait for it with patience.* ESV

It's a future hope!

Three Psychiatrists

In the period leading up to WW2 there were three Jewish psychiatrists, two learned masters in the field, and one young apprentice. The first master was a man named Sigmund Freud. He had spent years studying people, striving to understand what made people tick. He had reached the conclusion that the most basic drive in the human being was the drive for pleasure. He concluded that it is our need for pleasure that explains why we do what we do, how we live.

The second master was Alfred Adler. He too spent years studying human behavior. His studies led him to disagree with Sigmund Freud. Adler was convinced that the explanation for human behavior was power. We all grow up feeling inferior and powerless. He concluded that life was a drive to gain control, to feel we are important.

The third man was a young up-and-coming psychiatrist by the name of Victor Frankl. He hoped to follow in the footsteps of his mentors. But before his career gained any momentum WW2 started. The Nazis invaded and life became dangerous for Jews. Freud and Adler were world renowned scholars and managed to escape before Hitler invaded. Frankl was not so fortunate. He was arrested and thrown into a Nazi concentration camp for four long years.

After the war was over Frankl was released from the concentration camp and resumed his career. As he reflected upon his time as a prisoner, he observed something quite strange: the people who survived were not always the ones you'd expect. Many who were physically strong wasted away and died. Others who were weaker physically grew strong and survived. Why? What enabled them to hang on through a living hell?

Frankl reflected on the theories of his mentors. Freud's pleasure principle couldn't explain it. For four desperate and terrible years the men in that camp knew only pain, suffering, and degradation. Pleasure was a word absent from their vocabulary. It certainly wasn't pleasure that kept them going.

What then of Adler's theory about power being the basic human need? That didn't hold up well either. Frankl and his fellow Jews were completely powerless during their time in the concentration camps. Each day they stared down the barrel of loaded guns, were treated like animals, and felt jackboots on their faces. They had no power and no prospect of power.

Victor Frankl came up with his own theory. The difference between those who survived and those who perished was *hope*. Those who survived never gave up their belief that their lives had meaning. Despite everything going on around them, the suffering would one day end and they would again live meaningful, purposeful lives.

What is the basic human drive? What is the one thing that gives life value? The writer claims it is the ability to live with a sense of meaning or hope. Not pleasure. Not power. But some meaningful purpose.[3]

Meaning! Hope! Purpose!

The Shawshank Redemption

The Shawshank Redemption is a film that takes place in prison. It's the story of Andy Dufresne, who has been falsely convicted of his wife's murder. Life inside the prison was difficult. Red, a prisoner under a life sentence, befriended Andy and they both ultimately escaped. I will not spoil the story for those who have not seen the film, but the message of the film is clear:

Hope can set you free!

Discussion Questions

A. ZOPHAR'S FIRST SPEECH

A1. From Job 11:17-20, list the hope that Zophar described:

11:17

11:18

11:19

11:19

11:20

A2. Which one of these five hopeful occurrences in 11:17-20 do you think is the most important and why?

A3. What does it mean that "its darkness will be like morning"? (11:17)

A4. Why would it be important that "many will seek your favor" (11:19b)?

A5. Why do you think it is important that Zophar included verse 20?

Q. What if this were not true (there was no justice)?

A6. Is life with God always "brighter than the noonday?" (11:17)

A7. What does Zophar imply or say Job must do to receive the hopeful blessings he listed in 11:13-14?
Job 11:13 14   *If you prepare your heart, you will stretch out your hands toward him. 14 If iniquity is in your hand, put it far away, and let not injustice dwell in your tents.* ESV

Q. What is the underlying assumption behind Zophar's suggestions?

A8. How would you describe Zophar's theology relative to suffering (shared by the other two friends)?

A9. In your own words and view what were the three friends trying to accomplish with their words of hope?

B. JOB

B1. What was Job's state of mind in the following passages?
Job 7:6-7   *My days are swifter than a weaver's shuttle and come to their end* <u>without hope</u>. *7 Remember that my life is a breath; my eye will never again see good.* ESV

B2. What does 7:3 say about his state of mind before he made the above statement?
Job 7:3   *so I am allotted months of emptiness, and nights of misery are apportioned to me.* ESV

B3. Jumping ahead, after the three friends had made their first speeches, did Job's <u>state of mind</u> change? How would you describe Job in the following two passages?

Job 13:15-18   *Though he slay me, I will hope in him; yet I will argue my ways to his face. 16 This will be my salvation, that the godless shall not come before him. 17 Keep listening to my words, and let my declaration be in your ears. 18 Behold, I have prepared my case; I know that I shall be in the right.* ESV

Job 14:18-20   *But the mountain falls and crumbles away, and the rock is removed from its place; 19 the waters wear away the stones; the torrents wash away the soil of the earth; so you destroy the hope of man. 20 You prevail forever against him, and he passes; you change his countenance, and send him away.* ESV

B4. In Job 16-17 Elipaz replied to Job. Following are the last two verses of chapter 17. How is Job doing?

Job 17:15-16   *"Where then is my hope? Who will see my hope? 16 Will it go down to the bars of Sheol? Shall we descend together into the dust?"* ESV

B5. Bildad spoke again in chapter 18 and then Job said:
Job 19:8-10   *He has walled up my way, so that I cannot pass, and he has set darkness upon my paths. 9 He has stripped from me my glory and taken the crown from my head. 10 He breaks me down on every side, and I am gone, and my hope has he pulled up like a tree.* ESV

Q. Who is the "he" Job is referring to?

Q. How would you describe Job's view of his life status at this point?

C. BIBLICAL HOPE

In the end Job was restored (that's the rest of the story), but not because of his three friends. God's words to Job's three friends were: . . . *the Lord said to Eliphaz the Temanite: "My anger burns against you and against your two friends, for you have not spoken of me what is right, as my servant Job has* (Job 42:7). ESV

C1. Given 42:7 how would you describe the result of all the positive words Zophar did have to say? Did they carry the day?

C2. What do you think was the basic underlying cause of the ongoing unsupportive dialogue against Job?

Q. Where do we see this at work today?

C3. Where does hope come from?

C4. What do the following four passages from Proverbs tell us <u>not</u> to put our hope in?

11:7 _____
Proverbs 11:7   *When the wicked dies, his hope will perish, and the expectation of wealth perishes too.* ESV

11:23_____
Proverbs 11:23   *The desire of the righteous ends only in good; the expectation of the wicked in wrath.* ESV

23:17-18 _____
Proverbs 23:17-18   *Let not your heart envy sinners, but continue in the fear of the Lord all the day. 18 Surely there is a future, and your hope will not be cut off.* ESV

26:12_____
Proverbs 26:12   *Do you see a man who is wise in his own eyes? There is more hope for a fool than for him.* ESV

Q. Remember that proverbs are general, but not absolute, truths. Would your life experiences confirm all of these proverbs? Which one would you give an "Amen"? Why?

C5. What are the worldly things in which you might put your hope?

D. CHRISTIAN HOPE

The basic or foundational hope of all Christian believers is in God (Jesus):

> Ps 39:7   *And now, O Lord, for what do I wait? My* hope *is in you.* ESV
> Ps 62:5   *For God alone, O my soul, wait in silence, for my* hope *is from him.* ESV
> Matt 12:21   *and in his [Jesus] name the Gentiles will* hope." ESV

But the hope in God is not limited to the person of the divine godhead. The Christian has hope or faith in other important aspects of Christianity.

D1. Identify the object of our Christian hope in the following passages:

D1a. _____
Colossians 1:5   *because of the hope laid up for you in heaven. Of this you have heard before in the word of the truth, the gospel,* ESV

D1b. _____
1 Peter 1:13   *Therefore, preparing your minds for action, and being sober-minded, set your hope fully on the grace that will be brought to you at the revelation of Jesus Christ.* ESV

D1c. _____

Acts 24:15   *having a hope in God, which these men themselves accept, that there will be a resurrection of both the just and the unjust.* ESV

D1d. _____

Psalms 119:147   *I rise before dawn and cry for help; I hope in your words.* ESV

D1e. _____

Psalms 147:11   *but the Lord takes pleasure in those who fear him, in those who hope in his steadfast love.* ESV

D2. In Titus 3:6-7, what is the result of our hope in Christ?

Titus 3:6-7   *whom he poured out on us richly through Jesus Christ our Savior, 7 so that being justified by his grace we might become heirs according to the hope of eternal life.* ESV

E. APPLICATION

E1. Do you live your life with hope and joy? If not, why not?

E2. Can you testify to the importance of hope?

E3. Do you have hope in anything other than the grace of the Lord Jesus Christ? If so what is it and how is that working for you?

E4. Do you have serious concerns or doubts in the Gospel message? What is your concern? Can you honestly say that you believe the following?

> 1 Peter 1:3-9
> *Blessed be the God and Father of our Lord Jesus Christ! According to his great mercy, he has caused us to be born again to a living hope through the resurrection of Jesus Christ from the dead, 4 to an inheritance that is imperishable, undefiled, and unfading, kept in heaven for you, 5 who by God's power are being guarded through faith for a salvation ready to be revealed in the last time. 6 In this you rejoice, though now for a little while, if necessary, you have been grieved by various trials, 7 so that the tested genuineness of your faith—more precious than gold that perishes though it is tested by fire—may be found to result in praise and glory and honor at the revelation of Jesus Christ. 8 Though you have not seen him, you love him. Though you do not now see him, you believe in him and rejoice with joy that is inexpressible and filled with glory, 9 obtaining the outcome of your faith, the salvation of your souls.* ESV

And that's why we have HOPE!

Ten Virgins
who ran out of oil

Occurrences of these "virgins" in the Bible: 3
NOTE: The virgins are referenced a number of
additional times through the use of pronouns, etc.

Themes: Knowing God; Relationship; Parables

Scripture

<u>Mt 25:1-13</u>   <u>The Parable of the 10 Virgins</u>

Then the kingdom of heaven will be like ten virgins who took their lamps and went to meet the bridegroom. 2 Five of them were foolish, and five were wise. 3 For when the foolish took their lamps, they took no oil with them, 4 but the wise took flasks of oil with their lamps. 5 As the bridegroom was delayed, they all became drowsy and slept. 6 But at midnight there was a cry, 'Here is the bridegroom! Come out to meet him.' 7 Then all those virgins rose and trimmed their lamps. 8 And the foolish said to the wise, 'Give us some of your oil, for our lamps are going out.' 9 But the wise answered, saying, 'Since there will not be enough for us and for you, go rather to the dealers and buy for yourselves.' 10 And while they were going to buy, the bridegroom came, and those who were ready went in with him to the marriage feast, and the door was shut. 11 Afterward the other virgins came also, saying, 'Lord, lord, open to us.' 12 But he answered, 'Truly, I say to you, I do not know you.' 13 Watch therefore, for you know neither the day nor the hour. ESV

The Context

This parable occurs in the book of Matthew in a section addressing "end times" questions and issues. The story describes the kingdom of heaven and the nature of what will be true under the reign of Christ. It fits well with the other stories that Matthew recorded at the end of chapter 24:

> Keep Watch.
> Mt 24:42-44
> Warning that Jesus could come back at any time!

> Who is a Faithful and Wise Servant?
> Mt 24:45-51
> We have responsibilities in preparing for His coming. We cannot be passive.

The parable of the Ten Virgins fits naturally into this series of stories as it is focuses on being prepared for His coming even if there is a long delay.

Parables

Definition
Biblical parables are short, simple stories designed to communicate a spiritual truth, religious principle, or teach a moral lesson. They are stories in which truth is communicated by comparing examples drawn from everyday experiences. Often a vivid story is used to illustrate a life lesson, making it particularly useful for teaching. Biblical parables generally describe truths not then understood, even when plainly told (Luke 18:34).

Purpose
The purpose of the Biblical parable was both to hide and enlighten the truth. These stories revealed truth to the disciples and at the

same time concealed that truth from the rebellious Jews and Roman authorities. An uneducated Christian who had some understanding of the truth could quickly understand the teaching contained in the parable, but it would be absolutely confusing to the educated mind. Parables concealed the truth from those who did not have the true key to its hidden meaning. The uninformed often saw it as a tale or fantasy. Therefore, Jesus could teach His disciples the deep secrets of His kingdom, while others, who would have challenged the truth, heard the story without understanding.

The Nature of Parables

People often more easily understand a lesson presented through a story than an outline of facts. A story can be remembered easily while detailed explanations of doctrine, morals, or recommended lifestyle often quickly lose the listener's attention.

Parables have the following characteristics and implications:

(1) There is normally one main thought around which the entire story centers. Our objective should be to determine this primary teaching.

(2) The parable in its explanation or teaching must be easily understood and logical.

(3) Each parable has a specific scope or purpose.

(4) We should not look for special significance in every circumstance, situation, or detail in the parable.

(5) We must make a distinction between the primary purpose and the unimportant details in the story. These details serve only to set the scene and are not part of the purpose of the parable. Which details are significant and which are meaningless is often hard, sometimes almost impossible to determine.

(6) Jesus' direct teachings are the standard to which all interpretations and explanations must be compared. Biblical parables will not contradict Jesus' direct teaching.

(7) The parable should not constitute the primary source of doctrine. Doctrines may be illustrated, or more likely further confirmed, but it is not appropriate to determine doctrine first by the use of parables.

(8) The story may have multiple meanings or applications that might apply to the individual, the church, or both.[4]

Implications and Observations

The parable of the Ten Virgins uses some very significant language. When the virgins returned from getting more oil, the door was closed to them. This is a somewhat shocking end to this parable. The door is shut and the unprepared virgins (bridesmaids) are not allowed entrance. The bridegroom (representing Jesus) said he did not _know_ them. Therefore, *knowing* Christ is an absolute essential ingredient in our Christian walk. Otherwise, we are in danger of being turned away because there is no relationship. He does not know us. The "knowing" that is described here is heart knowledge, not head knowledge. It implies a personal relationship with God. God knows me because I am up every morning talking to Him in prayer and He in turn is talking to me through His Word.

The importance of knowing God is also pointed out in the Old Testament. In the book of Jeremiah we find this passage about boasting:

> Jeremiah 9:23-24   *Thus says the Lord: "Let not the wise man boast in his wisdom, let not the mighty man boast in his might, let not the rich man boast in his riches, 24 but let him who boasts boast in this, that he understands and knows me, that I am the Lord who practices steadfast love, justice, and righteousness in the earth. For in these things I delight, declares the Lord."* ESV

God says that if we are going to boast about anything, boast about underline knowing Him. My life is what it is because Christ is in my life. Nothing else really matters because my home or citizenship is not on this earth. I am just traveling through this life for a short time and the only thing of value I possess is my relationship with Christ. He knows me and I know Him.

Discussion Questions

<u>A. GENERAL</u>

A1. In this parable who is represented by:

a) the five wise virgins:

b) the five foolish virgins:

c) the bridegroom:

A2. Based on 25:1, what is the purpose of the parable?

A3. What are the primary teaching points of the parable?

A4. Do you think this parable means that few will enter the kingdom?

A5. The unprepared virgins are described as "foolish." What does that word mean to you?

A6. How would you contrast the qualities or nature of the five wise virgins and those who ran out of oil?

A7. Why didn't the foolish virgins get extra oil when they saw the extra oil of the wise virgins?

A8. Do you think it was unfair or selfish that the five virgins with extra oil did not share?

A9. In the context of what this parable is teaching, what would it mean for the wise virgins to warn the foolish ones to get more oil?

A10. Is there spiritual meaning to the wise virgins not sharing oil?

A11. What personal character attributes are present in today's society that are in conflict with this Biblical truth?

A12. What does this parable teach the person who thinks he can wait until late in life to make a decision about Christ (to be prepared), or put off the question until a later time when it is more convenient?

A13. What do you think it means "to be prepared"?

A14. Do you think it was "fair" that the bridegroom closed the door and would not permit others who wanted to enter to come into the celebration?

A15. If closing the door is shutting out unprepared sinners from heaven, do you think that is something a loving God would do?

B. KNOWING GOD

The passage in Mt 25:12 speaks about God knowing us. The reality and implication of that relationship is determined by how well we know God. It is not about knowing things about God, but having an intimate, growing, right relationship with Him. The nature of the relationship (the "knowing") is determined by how well we know God. Therefore, in this passage when it says that God does not know us, it means that we do not know Him.

B1. In Mt 25:12 the bridegroom (representing God or Jesus) says he does not know the latecomers and the door will remain shut. What do you think it means to _know_ God? Job answered this question in Job 22:21-30:

Come to terms with God and be at peace; in this way good will come to you. 22 Receive instruction from His mouth, and place His sayings in your heart. 23 If you return to the Almighty, you will be renewed. If you banish injustice from your tent 24 and consign your gold to the dust, the gold of Ophir to the stones in the wadis, 25 the Almighty will be your gold and your finest silver. 26 Then you will delight in the Almighty and lift up your face to God. 27 You will pray to Him, and He will hear you, and you will fulfill your vows. 28 When you make a decision, it will be carried out, and light will shine on your ways. 29 When others are humiliated and you say, "Lift them up," God will save the humble. 30 He will even rescue the guilty one, who will be rescued by the purity of your hands. HCSB

Q. How did Job describe the relationship in the following verses:

22:21 _____.
22:22 _____.
22:23 _____.
22:24-26 _____.
22:27_____.
22:29-30 _____.

B2. Do you think it is possible that the teaching point is not the concept of "knowing God" (or God knowing us), but that it is simply that the foolish ones did not plan well and were simply lazy or complacent?

B3. There are four major concepts or principles that demonstrate that we know God!

#1. What major principle do we learn from these two verses about knowing Christ?

> 1 John 2:3   *We know that we have come to know him if we obey his commands.*
> 1 John 2:6   *Whoever claims to live in him must walk as Jesus did.*

> Answer:

#2. What do we learn in the following about knowing God? What act demonstrates that we know Him?

> 1 John 4:7-8   *Beloved, let us love one another, for love is from God, and whoever loves has been born of God and knows God. 8 Anyone who does not love does not know God, because God is love.* ESV

> 1 Corinthians 8:1-3   *Now concerning food offered to idols: we know that "all of us possess knowledge." This "knowledge" puffs up, but love builds up. 2 If anyone*

imagines that he knows something, he does not yet know as he ought to know. 3 But if anyone loves God, he is known by God. ESV

Answer:

#3. Based on John 15:4-5, how do we know that we know Him? How is the intimate relationship described?

John 15:4-6   *Abide in me, and I in you. As the branch cannot bear fruit by itself, unless it abides in the vine, neither can you, unless you abide in me. 5 I am the vine; you are the branches. Whoever abides in me and I in him, he it is that bears much fruit, for apart from me you can do nothing. ESV*

Answer:

#4. What is the requirement for knowing God in the following:

Titus 1:16   *They profess to know God, but they deny him by their works. They are detestable, disobedient, unfit for any good work. ESV*

Answer:

C. REQUIREMENTS FOR BEING A DISCIPLE

C1. Based on the following what are the requirements for being a disciple of Jesus?

#1 What is the requirement in John 8:31?
"If you hold to my teaching, you are really my disciples."

      Answer:

#2 What is the requirement in John 13:35?
"By this all men will know that you are my disciples, if you love one another."

      Answer:

#3 What is the requirement in John 15:8?
". . . that you bear much fruit, showing yourselves to be my disciples."

      Answer:

C2. What conclusions can you draw by comparing C1 and B3?

D. APPLICATION

A *saving relationship* with God is a right relationship, not a list of accomplishments or a standard of behavior that must be achieved. This is dramatically illustrated by another passage in Scripture that can be very frightening if not understood correctly:

> Matthew 7:21-23   *"Not everyone who says to me, 'Lord, Lord,' will enter the kingdom of heaven, but only he who does the will of my Father who is in heaven. 22 Many will*

> *say to me on that day, 'Lord, Lord, did we not prophesy in*
> *your name, and in your name drive out demons and*
> *perform many miracles?' 23 Then I will tell them plainly,*
> *'I never knew you. Away from me, you evildoers!'"*

Here is someone who prophesied in Jesus' name, drove out demons, and performed many miracles, but did not have a personal relationship with the Lord. Jesus says, "I never knew you." At first glance one might conclude that if a person who does all this (in Jesus' name) still cannot get into heaven, what chance do I have? But the issue is not this man's performance. The problem is that he did not have a relationship with Christ, because Christ did not _know_ him. The lack of a personal relationship is what kept him out of heaven.

In many ways this understanding should be a great relief to us, because typically our performance activity leaves a lot to be desired. This passage confirms the foundational calling on all Jesus-followers: I am a Christian because I have a personal relationship with God through Christ. Jesus-followers do not do good works in order to be "saved," rather, we do them out of the overflow or excess of the love relationship that develops with Christ.

Good works are not a requirement in order that Jesus "knows" us. Rather, they are acts of gratitude performed because we are grateful and thankful that God's justice has been replaced with His mercy and grace.

The bottom line is that it does _not_ matter how many good deeds we do or how spectacular they might be (e.g. casting out demons). If we have no personal relationship with Christ the doors to the celebration (Kingdom) are closed. Therefore, first and foremost, we must be concerned that Jesus knows us; that we have a personal *relationship* with Christ.

That means:

- We obey God.
- We love God and others.
- We abide in Christ.
- We produce fruit.

D1. In addition to knowing Jesus, The Parable of the Ten Virgins teaches us that we must always be prepared for His coming. We cannot be lazy or complacent because that is not the desired status Jesus wants from His followers.

Are you prepared?

D2. Another understanding we gain from this parable is that others cannot cover for our unfaithfulness. The five virgins with excess oil only had enough for themselves. Each person must be responsible for his own relationship with God. There are no second chances once the door is closed.

Have you taken responsibility?

D3. How do you want Jesus to find you when He returns? What do you think Jesus expects or desires of His people when He returns?

> Matt 24:45-46   *Who then is the faithful and wise servant, whom his master has set over his household, to give them their food at the proper time? 46 Blessed is that servant whom his master will find so doing when he comes.* ESV

Are you ready?

D4. In the real world (your life) what gets in the way of knowing Christ?

- What gets in the way of following His commands?
- What gets in the way of loving God and loving others?
- What gets in the way of abiding in Christ and He in you?
- What gets in the way of producing fruit?
- What gets in the way of your prayer life?
- What gets in the way of your serving in the church?

What's in your way?

The Samaritans
listened to woman at well

Occurrences of "Samaritans" in John 4: 3

Themes: Living Water; Personal Testimony; Personal Encounter; Personal Belief

---

Scripture

John 4:10, 13-14, 28-30, 39-42
Jesus answered her, "If you knew the gift of God, and who it is that is saying to you, 'Give me a drink,' you would have asked him, and he would have given you living water." . . . 13 Jesus said to her, "Everyone who drinks of this water will be thirsty again, 14 but whoever drinks of the water that I will give him will never be thirsty forever. The water that I will give him will become in him a spring of water welling up to eternal life."

28 So the woman left her water jar and went away into town and said to the people, 29 "Come, see a man who told me all that I ever did. Can this be the Christ?" 30 They went out of the town and were coming to him.

39 Many Samaritans from that town believed in him because of the woman's testimony, "He told me all that I ever did." 40 So when the Samaritans came to him, they asked him to stay with them, and he stayed there two days. 41 And many more believed because of his word. 42 They said to the woman, "It is no longer because of what you said that we believe, for we have heard for ourselves, and we know that this is indeed the Savior of the world." ESV

The Context

Jesus was heading north from Judea, probably from the Judean countryside (John 3:22) after leaving Jerusalem. Because he was traveling toward Galilee which is north of Samaria, the quickest and most direct route was through Samaria. Jews typically didn't travel through Samaria because of their great hatred of the Samaritans who were considered traitors and "permanently unclean."

The text indicates that Jesus was tired (being fully human) and He sat down at the well. Jacob's well was located in Samaria near a town called Sychar. Around noon, a local Samaritan woman arrived to draw water from the well and Jesus asked her if she would give Him a drink. This would not have been acceptable behavior for any good Jew. In the ensuing conversation with the woman, Jesus made several startling statements:

- He could give her living water.
- Everyone who drank water from Jacob's Well would get thirsty again, but the water He would give would become a well of water "springing up to eternal life."
- A time was coming when true worshipers would worship the Father (who was Spirit) in spirit and truth.

In the conversation, the woman said, *"I know that Messiah is coming (he who is called Christ). When He comes, he will tell us all things."* (John 4:25). Jesus responded, *"I who speak to you am he."* (John 4:26). The woman then left the water jar she had brought to the well and went back into the town to tell the men about what had happened.

The woman's reputation was not one that would give credibility to her story. She came to the well alone, without any other women, at a time of day when people were not likely to be around. This is a hint about her lifestyle and relationships with the other women in the village. Normally the women came together at the well in the morning. It was a social event. The fact that she was alone probably indicates she had few friends or that she was being shunned by the women of the town.

She might have been an outcast because of her marital situation (having multiple husbands and living with a man not her husband). The text doesn't tell us her exact reputation, but all reasonable indications are that it was not good. Her lifestyle would have automatically put her in a class of immoral, damaged, and undesirable women.

Neither do we really know what she told the townspeople. We do know the result. Her story was obviously effective because, "Many Samaritans from that town believed in Him because of the woman's testimony" (4:39).

The Samaritans

The Samaritans could be described as half-Jew and half-Gentile. After Assyria invaded the northern kingdom of Israel in 721 BC, many Jewish people were exiled to Assyria, but some of the Jews remained in Israel. Those who remained intermarried with the invading Assyrians and native pagan peoples. The resulting religious belief system became a combination of Jewish customs and pagan beliefs.

The Samaritans had their own temple, their own Torah (the first five books of the Old Testament), and their own religious system and worship practices. Because of these impure practices, they were rejected or shunned by the Jews as half-breeds, foreigners, outcasts, pagans, and unclean. During the time of Jesus' ministry the Jews and Samaritans avoided contact and did not even speak to one another. The relationship was so bad that the Jews would make extreme efforts not to touch foot in Samaria. They would typically cross the Jordan and travel between Judea and Galilee on the east side of the Jordan River, increasing the length of their trip, but avoiding any contact with the unclean Samaritans.

Discussion Questions

A. THE STORY

A1. The text says the woman went back to town and told the "men" what had happened. Why only the men? Do you think that means she did not tell any of the women?

A2. Do you think the woman had credibility with the townspeople?

A3. Did the woman tell her "husband" (the man she was living with)? Assuming the woman did not tell him about Jesus first, why not?

A4. What is the significance, if any, of the woman leaving her water jug at the well?

A5. What was the woman's testimony to the men?

A6. Why did the Samaritans believe, given she was a woman and had a poor reputation?

A7. Given that "many" Samaritans believed, why did Jesus stay for only two days? Why would Jesus leave the Samaritans on their own?

A8. Why did the men tell the woman they no longer believed just based on her testimony (4:42)?

A9. What three things are particularly significant in 4:42b, "*we have heard for ourselves and know that this is indeed the Savior of the world?*" (ESV)

(a)

(b)

(c)

A10. How do you think this overwhelming understanding occurred? This seems like a very big leap.

A11. Why did Jesus reveal He was the Messiah? This is really the only time that Jesus says that He is the Messiah (although Mk 9:41 comes close). Why do you suspect that Jesus revealed this in Samaria and not in Jerusalem?

A12. Jesus spent two days with the Samaritans. What does that say about the Jewish custom of shunning the Samaritans?

A13. Can you think of any other examples in Scripture when Jesus did not conform to common Jewish customs?

A14. Why do you think Jesus traveled through Samaria? John 4:4 says, "*He had to pass through Samaria*." This implies some bigger purpose than just the quickest way to reach Galilee.

A15. Jesus spoke to one person (the woman at the well) and that one conversation led many Samaritans from the town to belief. Do you find this result normal or an exception to normal experience?

A16. Can you think of any example in our society today where Christians refuse to go through "Samaria"?

A17. What is the nature of the people in Samaria to whom He revealed Himself? Who would you have chosen?

B. LIVING WATER

B1. Given the following, do you think the woman and the townspeople knew the implications of what Jesus said about "living water" in John 4:10-14?

- Isa 12:3   *With joy you will draw water from the wells of salvation.* ESV
- Jer 2:13   *for my people have committed two evils: they have forsaken me, the fountain of living waters, and hewed out cisterns for themselves, broken cisterns that can hold no water.* ESV
- Jer 17:13   *. . . for they have forsaken the Lord, the fountain of living water.* ESV
- Isa 55:1   *Come, everyone who thirsts, come to the waters; . . .* ESV

B2. In this passage (4:10-14), who is giving the water and what is its significance?

C. APPLICATION

C1. Do you have His living water? Given the above understanding of living water, what does the following confirm?

> Rev 7:16-17   *They shall hunger no more, neither thirst anymore; the sun shall not strike them, nor any scorching heat. 17 For the Lamb in the midst of the throne will be their shepherd, and he will guide them to springs of living water, and God will wipe away every tear from their eyes.* ESV

C2. The townspeople confirmed their own personal belief after meeting Jesus. They did not depend on the woman's testimony alone. We must all have a personal encounter with Jesus to be born again. We enter the Kingdom not because of our family, our church, or by saying a prayer. We enter the Kingdom through a personal relationship with Christ. What is the status of your relationship?

C3. How effective is your testimony? Do you need to work on your story?

- How can you make your testimony more effective?
- Have you updated your story lately?
- Are you as excited about your testimony, as the woman at the well?
- Our only responsibility is to tell, so God can use our story.

C4. Who do you avoid or shun because of their reputation, lifestyle, social standing, geographic location, language, culture, health, denomination, race, or sexual orientation? Why?

Transformation Road Map
Primary Takeaways

1: We should demonstrate unwavering obedience to God's instructions, even in the face of challenging and unconventional circumstances.

2: Genuine repentance and faith in Jesus lead to profound gratitude, expressed through humble acts of worship and love, regardless of one's past sins or social status.

3: We must humbly submit to God's sovereign will and allow Him to shape our lives according to His purposes, even when it involves difficult changes or challenges.

4: God demands complete honesty and integrity in our dealings with Him and His church, as deception and hypocrisy can have severe consequences for both individuals and the community of believers.

5: Bold, humble, and faith-filled prayers for God's blessing, guidance, and protection are pleasing to Him and can lead to His provision and favor when aligned with His will.

6: While offering comfort and hope to those suffering is commendable, we must be cautious not to make hasty judgments about the reasons for their trials or offer simplistic solutions based on incomplete understanding of God's ways.

7: Believers must remain spiritually vigilant and prepared for Christ's return by maintaining a genuine and active relationship with Him through the Holy Spirit.

8: Jesus offers living water - the Holy Spirit and eternal life - to all people regardless of their background, social status, or past sins, and those who receive it can become powerful witnesses for Christ.

Free PDF
MAKE WISE DECISIONS

[Get the ebook version for 99 cents]

Consequences Shape Lives.

This book discusses the nature of decisions and explores eight essential questions to make better decisions.

You are a few decisions away from transforming your life. You can make better decisions! This resource has sections on what makes a poor decision, questions to ask yourself, traps to avoid, short and sweet decisions, the wise decision framework, and twenty ways to be wise. It also has a handy decision-making checklist. (12 pages)

Free PDF: https://getwisdompublishing.com/resource-registration/

Kindle ebook for 99 cents: https://www.amazon.com/dp/B0FG8NC53J

Ebook

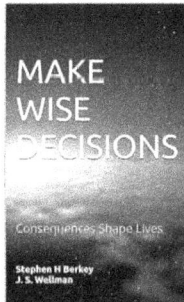

MAKE WISE DECISIONS

Consequences Shape Lives

Stephen H Berkey
J. S. Wellman

Free PDF

Ten Steps to Wise Choices

Timeless Wisdom. Practical Tools. Lasting Impact.

Free PDF
Life Improvement Principles
[Get the ebook version for 99 cents]

You can live your best life!

Welcome to a journey of discovery! In case you have forgotten, your actions have consequences. Unlock your potential! This book (60+ pages) provides the overview of all our strategies and wisdom principles to live your best life. You *can* transform your life! Get your wisdom-based roadmap to a better life and unlock all the possibilities for growth and success.

Free PDF: https://getwisdompublishing.com/resource-registration/

Kindle ebook for 99 cents:
https://www.amazon.com/dp/B0FG883KZM

Ebook

Free PDF

Make it your life goal to be the best you can be!

Discover Wisdom and live the life you deserve.

Next Steps!

Continue Studying the *OBSCURE* Series
The *OBSCURE* Bible Study Series
https://www.amazon.com/dp/B08T7TL1B1

Be Challenged by the Jesus Follower Series
The Jesus Follower Bible Study Series
https://www.amazon.com/dp/B0DHP39P5J

Tackle Wisdom-Driven Life Change
Apply Biblical Wisdom to Live Your Best Life!
"Effective Life Change"
https://www.amazon.com/dp/1952359732

Know What You Should Pray
Personal Daily Prayer Guide
https://www.amazon.com/What-Should-Pray-Personal-Journal/dp/1952359260/

Decide to be the Very Best You Can Be
The Life Planning Series
https://www.amazon.com/dp/B09TH9SYC4

You Can Help:
SOCIAL MEDIA: Mention The *OBSCURE* Bible Study Series on your social platforms. Include the hashtag #obscurebiblestudy so we are aware of your post.

FRIENDS: Recommend *OBSCURE* to your family, friends, small group, Sunday School class leaders, or your church.

REVIEW: Please give us your honest review at
https://www.amazon.com/dp/195235904X

The *OBSCURE* Bible Study Series

Continue your journey through the hidden wisdom of Scripture with the OBSCURE Series.

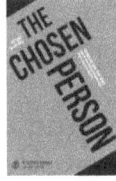

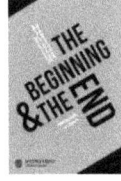

Blasphemy, Grace, Quarrels & Reconciliation: The lives of first-century disciples.
This book presents Joseph of Arimathea, Joanna, Ananias, Hymenaeus, and Cornelius (a centurion). It illustrates the nature and challenges of life as a first-century disciple.

The Beginning and the End: From creation to eternity.
This book has four lessons from Genesis and four from Revelation covering creation, rebellion, grace, worship, and eternity. God is leading us to worship in the Throne Room.

God at the Center: He is sovereign and I am not.
This book examines the virgin birth, worship, prayer, the sovereignty of God, compromise, and trust. God is at the center of all these stories. He is at the center of our lives.

Women of Courage: God did some serious business with these women.
This book examines the lives of Jael, Rizpah, the woman of Tekoa, Tabitha, Shiphrah, and Lydia. These women exhibit great courage and faithfulness. God used them in amazing ways.

The Beginning of Wisdom: Your personal character counts.
In this book we find courage, loyalty, thankfulness, love, forgiveness, and humility. Personal character counts. Decisions have consequences. Wisdom will help us stand firm in our faith.

Miracles & Rebellion: The good, the bad, and the indifferent.
God hates sin and loves to heal the faithful. The rebellion of Korah, Haman, and Alexander compare to the healing stories of Aeneas, a slave girl, and the crippled man at Lystra.

The Chosen People: There is a remnant.
This book concentrates mostly on Israel in the Old Testament, but also covers some interesting subjects as Lucifer, Michael the archangel, and Job's wife.

The Chosen Person: Keep your eyes on Jesus.
The focus is on Jesus and the superiority of Christ. We investigate Melchizedek, the disciples on the road to Emmaus, Nicodemus, and the criminal on the cross.

WEBSITE: http://getwisdompublishing.com/products/
AMAZON: www.amazon.com/author/stephenhberkey

Jesus Follower Bible Study Series

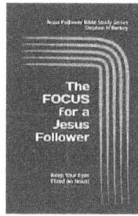

The Jesus Follower Bible Study Series will provide you with a complete description of the nature, characteristics, obligations, commitments, and responsibilities of a true Jesus follower.

Go to our Amazon Book Series page for your copy:
https://www.amazon.com/dp/B0DHP39P5J

The RELATIONSHIP CHARACTERISTICS of a Jesus Follower:
> Are you right with God?

The ONE ANOTHER INSTRUCTIONS to a Jesus Follower:
> Are you right with one another?

The WORSHIP of a Jesus Follower:
> Is your worship acceptable or in vain?

The PRAYER of a Jesus Follower:
> What Scripture says about unleashing the power of God.

The DANGERS of SIN for a Jesus Follower:
> God HATES sin! He abhors sin!

The FOCUS for a Jesus Follower:
> Keep your eyes fixed on Jesus!

The HEART Requirements of a Jesus Follower:
> Follow with all your heart, mind, body, and soul!

The COMMITMENTS of a Jesus Follower:
> Practical Christian living and discipleship.

The OBEDIENCE Requirements for a Jesus Follower:
> Ignore at your own risk!

"Get Wisdom Publishing creates wisdom-driven products that equip readers with timeless insights, understanding, and actionable tools to transform their lives."

Life Planning Series

Read these books if you want to live a better life.
The primary audience for this series is the secular self-help market, but the concepts are Christian based.

CHOOSE FAITH	**For the spiritual seeker and those with spiritual questions.** *Your Spiritual Guidebook For Questions About Religion, God, Heaven, Truth, Evil, and the Afterlife.* https://www.amazon.com/dp/1952359473
CHOOSE CORE VALUES	**Core values will drive your life.** https://www.amazon.com/dp/195235949X

Other Titles in the Life Planning Series
CHOOSE Integrity
CHOOSE Friends Wisely
CHOOSE The Right Words
CHOOSE Good Work Habits
CHOOSE Financial Responsibility
CHOOSE A Positive Self-Image
CHOOSE Leadership
CHOOSE Love and Family
LIFE PLANNING HANDBOOK A Life Plan Is The Key To Personal Growth https://www.amazon.com/gp/product/1952359325

Go to:
https://www.amazon.com/dp/B09TH9SYC4
to get these books.

Personal Daily Prayer Guide
Prayer Resource and Journal

This is a great resource to kick-start your prayer life!

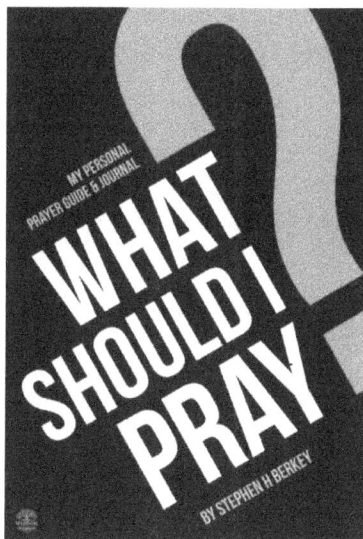

Know what to pray.
Pray based on Bible verses.
Strengthen your prayer life.
Access reference resources.
Pray with eternal implications.
Write your own prayers if desired.
Organize and focus your prayer time.
Learn what the Bible says about prayer.
Find encouragement and advice on how to pray.
Reduce frustration and distraction in your prayer time.

Get your copy today!

https://www.amazon.com/What-Should-Pray-Personal-Journal/dp/1952359260/

Acknowledgments

Arlene
Arlene has served as wife, editor, and proof-reader for all of my writing – thank you for your patience, help, and love.

Michelle
Michelle, our older daughter, has been an invaluable resource. She has graciously produced the website at www.getwisdompublishing.com. She was the first author in the family: graceandthegravelroad.com.

Stephanie
Our middle daughter designed all the covers for the *OBSCURE* Bible Study Series, as well as the marks and logos for Get Wisdom Publishing. We are grateful for her talent!

KOINONIA Small Group
These dear friends have hung in there with me as I taught many of the lessons to them first. Their input, answers, and suggestions have been invaluable.

God, Jesus, and Holy Spirit
Thank you, Lord, for Your guidance and direction.

Notes

1 DVD: "*In the Potter's Hands*," with Pastor Pat Lazovich, recorded live at Calvary Chapel of Costa Mesa, CA

2 Nelson's Illustrated Bible Dictionary, Copyright © 1986, Thomas Nelson Publishers; from PC Study Bible, "Sanctification"

3 Nelson's Illustrated Bible Dictionary, Copyright © 1986, Thomas Nelson Publishers; from PC Study Bible, "Hope"

4 From a talk given by Australian speaker Michael Frost.

5 This list of the characteristics of parables is a summary, paraphrase, or interpretation of a number of different sources and writings on this subject, none of which can be specifically identified.

6 International Standard Bible Encyclopedia, revised edition, Copyright © 1979 by Wm. B. Eerdmans Publishing Co.; from PC Study Bible, "Fool" All rights reserved.

7 Nelson's Illustrated Bible Dictionary, Copyright © 1986, Thomas Nelson Publishers; from PC Study Bible, "Fool"

About the Author

Steve attended church as a child and accepted Christ when he was 10 years old. But his walk with Jesus left a lot to be desired for the next 44 years. In 1994 he "wrestled" with God for some period of months and in September of that year totally surrendered his life to Jesus.

In 1996 he was so driven to study God's Word that he attended the Indianapolis campus of Trinity Evangelical Divinity School (Chicago) to earn a Certificate of Biblical Studies. His hunger for God's Word led him to lead and write all his own Bible studies for his small group. He has been an entrepreneur and Bible study leader for the past 30 years.

He is a member of The Church at Station Hill in Spring Hill, TN, a regional campus of Brentwood Baptist (Brentwood TN).

Contact Us

Website: www.getwisdompublishing.com

Email: info@getwisdompublishing.com

Facebook: Get Wisdom Publishing

Author's Page: www.amazon.com/author/stephenhberkey

Amazon's Obscure Bible Study Series page:
https://www.amazon.com/dp/B08T7TL1B1

"Go beyond devotionals.
Experience biblical wisdom in action!"

GET**WISDOM**
P U B L I S H I N G

www.ingramcontent.com/pod-product-compliance
Lightning Source LLC
Chambersburg PA
CBHW070811050426
42452CB00011B/1988